LETTING THE LIGHT IN

How A Baby With Down Syndrome Changed My Life

Karen Lawrence

For my family, with gratitude and love.

You broke me open
You shattered my perfection
You let the light in.

CONTENTS

Title Page

Copyright

Dedication

Epigraph

Foreword

Chapter One: Another Baby   1

Chapter Two: Annus Horribilis   6

Chapter Three: Is There A Problem?   12

Chapter Four: A Narrow Room   19

Chapter Five: The Phone Call   25

Chapter Six: Dark Places   30

Chapter Seven: Telling People   36

Chapter Eight: The Changeling and the Moon   42

Chapter Nine: She's Not Growing   48

Chapter Ten: Blessings, prayers and fears   54

Chapter Eleven: A Summer of Waiting   60

Chapter Twelve: Heart Surgery   66

Chapter Thirteen: Hospital Stay   71

Chapter Fourteen: Growing and Learning   76

Chapter Fifteen: You Only Have To Love This Child   82

Chapter Sixteen: Christmas Confession   87

Chapter Seventeen: Communication and Confidence   92

Chapter Eighteen: Family Impact   97

Chapter Nineteen: School Days   103

Chapter Twenty: We Are All Disabled   110

Chapter Twenty-one: Letting the Light In   115

Postscript: To Test or Not To Test?   122

About The Author   135

Books By This Author   137

FOOTNOTES AND FURTHER READING   139

FOREWORD

Thank you so much for picking up this little book.

Just a few quick words about what this book is *not*. It is not a guide to caring for a child with Down Syndrome, or an explanation of the condition. Other people have written about that far better than I can.

This book does not set out to see things from anyone's point of view other than my own. This is not my family's story. It is not even Martha's story. It is only my story. I have simply tried my best to be honest in recalling the impact Martha's arrival and early years had on me.

I am well aware that many people cope with significantly greater challenges than I do. Many children have more severe disabilities than Martha. Many parents live in more difficult circumstances. All I have to offer is my account of what happened to me, in the hope that it might be helpful to someone.

A quick note on terminology. The medical term for Martha's condition is *Trisomy 21*, so named because a person with Down Syndrome has a third, extra chromosome 21. The syndrome was identified in the 1860s by the English doctor, John Langdon Down. He named the condition

Mongolian idiocy, but by the 1960s this term was dropped as offensive. *Down's Syndrome* was adopted as an alternative.[1]

The terms *Down's Syndrome, Downs Syndrome* and *Down Syndrome* are all in common use today, alongside *Trisomy 21.* Writers in the USA tend to favour *Down Syndrome,* while *Down's Syndrome* or *Downs Syndrome* tend to be more prevalent in the UK. Some people take the view that the possessive *Down's* should not be used as it suggests incorrectly that the condition belongs to Dr Langdon Down.

In this book I have chosen to use *Down Syndrome* mostly for simplicity. I feel that too many s's and apostrophes tend to complicate things. But I do not have a problem with *Down's* or *Downs* as alternatives, and I have used these terms when quoting from writers or organisations who use them.

I have tried throughout to use 'people first' language. This means referring, for example, to 'a baby with Down Syndrome' and not 'a Downs baby', or 'a Downs'. The language we use shapes our thinking. It is important to recognise that all people with disabilities are people first, and should not be defined by a condition.[2] The only exception to this is where I have recalled my own or other people's actual words or thoughts.

I would add, however, that language changes all the time. Terms which are acceptable, even enlightened, today may be seen as offensive tomorrow. I have done my best to be respectful and consistent, but please bear with me. I believe it is more important to treat one another with genuine kindness than to worry too much about 'correct' use of words and definitions.

Some of the proceeds from the sale of this book will be donated to the UK Down's Syndrome Association.

I hope you enjoy reading it.

CHAPTER ONE: ANOTHER BABY

I had other plans for that day. The baby wasn't due for another two weeks. It was a Saturday morning, and I was going to take Jerome and Verity, aged four and three, to a friend's birthday party at a local soft play centre. So the regular tightenings in my belly were a definite inconvenience, if a little exciting too.

My caesarean section was booked for the 26th of January, just a few days before my forty-second birthday. This was my seventh baby, and I had already had two c-section births, so I had had no difficulty persuading my obstetrician to agree to a surgical delivery this time. To be honest, I preferred it this way. I was a busy mum who liked to be organised, so it was nice to have the birth neatly written into my diary. Everything was in order, the house clean and tidy, the baby clothes washed and ready in their drawers. Another baby would be easy. I had done this plenty of times before.

I ignored the squeezing sensations around my bump for an hour or two. Just Braxton Hicks, I told myself. It'll ease off soon. But by ten in the morning the gripping pains were coming regularly, every ten minutes or so. As I knelt down to clean the toilet, an unmistakable contraction swept over me, strong enough that I had to concentrate on breathing through it. OK, maybe this was the real thing.

I told Adrian, and then phoned the hospital. They told me to come in. Having my seventh baby meant I was categorised as a 'grand multipara' - someone who has had five or more previous births. This together with my age and previous c-sections made my pregnancy 'high risk' in hospital speak. I didn't see it that way, though. All my other babies had been fine, and I was fit and healthy. I wasn't expecting anything to go wrong.

I packed a couple of bags, cancelled the children's party plans, and drove myself to the hospital. The pains were still mild enough, though persistent, and Adrian would come and join me once he had sorted out the family at home. Nothing felt very urgent. None of my babies had arrived particularly quickly. I was an old hand at all this.

By the time Adrian arrived I was settled in an ante-natal bed, drinking tea and perusing a pile of magazines while awaiting my turn in theatre. A couple of paracetamol had taken the edge off the contractions. A midwife had examined me and pronounced me to be three centimetres dilated. My baby's heartbeat was fine, and my c-section would go ahead once the team were ready for me.

I had requested a transfer after the birth to the local low risk maternity unit. I intended to spend a few well-earned days recovering there, eating chocolate and relaxing in bed with my newborn. It would be a nice break from the responsibilities of home, and I hoped to linger there until the midwives turfed me out. Mothers of big families learn to grab whatever holidays they can wrangle!

It was mid-afternoon by the time Adrian and I made our way down to the operating theatre, suitably gowned and capped. I was familiar with the procedures from Jerome's and Verity's births. I sat on the edge of the high operating couch curled up over a pillow while the anaesthetist administered the spinal.

Then I was lying down, blood pressure cuff on my arm and a drip in the back of my hand. Adrian sat by my head, the screen went up to shield us from the view of my insides, and the surgeon appeared and introduced herself. A radio was playing music in the background. The medics were chatting calmly, the anaesthetist friendly at my side. Everything felt normal and safe.

Soon there was a rummaging and pulling sensation in my belly. I couldn't wait to see the baby now. Would it be a boy or a girl? I was quietly hoping for a girl this time, partly because I liked the name 'Martha' we had recently agreed on.

As I squeezed Adrian's hand the infant was lifted from me. Someone took it straight to the resuscitation trolley on the far side of the room. I didn't hear it cry at first, but I wasn't too worried. I knew babies sometimes needed a little help to start breathing, especially after a c-section. All of my other babies had been fine. I couldn't hear what the medics were saying over there by my baby, but I was sure everything would be fine.

'It's a little girl', someone told me. 'Doctor's just checking her over. You can see her in a moment.'

Sure enough the mewling wail of a newborn rang through the air. I realised I had been holding my own breath. Now I smiled and felt Adrian relax at my side.

'Can I see her?'

The midwife came over carrying a little bundle wrapped in a white NHS towel. A tiny pink face peeped out.

'Here's your baby', said the midwife.

I looked at my baby.
I knew instantly, the moment I saw her face.
I knew.

A voice in my head said,

'Oh. She's got Down Syndrome.'
But I didn't say it aloud.
No one said it aloud.
Everyone carried on as though nothing was wrong.

So I told myself I had imagined it.

If I didn't say it, or even think it,
perhaps it wouldn't be true.

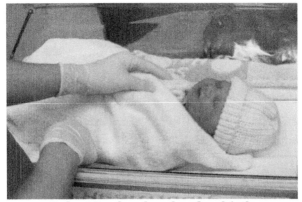

Baby Martha shortly after birth

CHAPTER TWO: ANNUS HORRIBILIS

When I tell someone we have seven children I will usually get one (or more) of the following reactions:

'*How* many?!'

'Oh my God, you must be superwoman!'

'Are you out of your mind?'

'Did you plan to have that many?'

'Are you Catholic?'

And my replies:

'Yep. Seven. All mine and my husband's.'

'No, I'm definitely not superwoman. But I am quite an organised person, and I did always enjoy being pregnant.'

'No idea whether or not I'm crazy. But in plenty of cultures it isn't so unusual.'

'Planned? No, not really. Not from the outset anyway. But we love our children and have been blessed to be able to provide for them.'

'And yes I am Catholic, as it happens. But it's probably less straightforward than you imagine.' (More about that later.)

Having a larger than average family kept me busy, but it didn't seem unreasonably difficult. I had uncomplicated pregnancies and healthy babies. Our children were well spaced out in age. By the time baby number six, Verity, arrived everything seemed to be going smoothly.

All the children seemed happy, and the older ones were getting excellent school reports. Adrian had a well-paid job in the City and we had recently moved to a smart five bedroom house in a nice part of Essex. I had gratefully given up my demanding job as a tax consultant to enjoy the luxury of being a full-time mum. I felt confident, successful and maybe a little smug.

Then came 2006.

Queen Elizabeth II called 1992 her 'annus horribilis' as she recalled a year in which her family was scarred by divorce, scandal and a devastating fire. Adrian and I experienced our personal 'annus horribilis' in 2006, the year before Martha was born.

It began in January with the sudden death of Adrian's father. Shortly after that, Adrian's grieving mother was diagnosed with breast cancer. In the ensuing maelstrom of emotions I fell pregnant, but a couple of months later I lost the baby to miscarriage. This hit me hard. We hadn't planned to have a seventh child, but now I was desperate to try again. Adrian wasn't so keen.

We organised a holiday to recover, but just as we were about to get onto the plane I received a phone call to tell me my own Dad had died. And then, not long after this blow, Adrian was made redundant from his job. Feeling the pressure of a large family to support, he rushed to find another role. But the experience had knocked his confidence and he wasn't happy in his new position.

I remember changing my ring tone on my phone that year because I had come to associate the old chimes with news of disaster. By the end of 2006 we were reeling from what felt like a merciless series of shocks, desperate for some peace and calm.

But in the middle of all this misery I harboured a precious hope. I was pregnant again. This time the pregnancy seemed to be growing normally, and as the months rolled on the new baby came to signify a fresh start. After all the death and loss, surely we deserved something good. 2007 would be a better year. It had to be.

I relished being pregnant. It always made me feel special, carrying new life inside me. I knew this would be our last baby, and I wanted to make the most of every moment. Perhaps it was this that made me almost relentless in my optimism that nothing could go wrong. I had a few moments of doubt, but I was adept at pushing them away.

I recall one afternoon in late summer. I must have been four or five months pregnant. All the children were at school or nursery, and I was sitting in the garden enjoying a cup of tea. The sun was warm on my skin and I breathed in the scent of lavender and marigolds from the pots at my side. The baby wriggled about inside me. I loved this peaceful time before the frantic pace of the school run.

This particular afternoon I was reading a magazine article about family life written by a mother of nine children. The youngest child in this woman's family had Down Syndrome. The writer described how this child had experienced various health problems, but had become an unexpected blessing.

My skin suddenly turned cold, despite the sunshine. For a moment or two I contemplated the possibility. What if that happens to us? What if our baby has Down Syndrome? How could I cope with a child who might have constant infections, heart problems, poor vision, behavioural issues and sleep disturbances, to say nothing of severe learning delays? I had six children to deal with already. It would be an unthinkable disaster.

I knew the statistics. I knew that the probability of having a child with a chromosomal disorder such as Down Syndrome rises steeply after a mother reaches the age of forty. I always used to say I would not have a baby after my fortieth birthday for that very reason. But I had not anticipated our annus horribilis and my aching need to replace the pregnancy lost through miscarriage.

Adrian had raised the risk of Down Syndrome as one of his reasons for wanting to stop at six children, but I had blithely replied that it was unlikely to happen to us. I reasoned to myself that my 1 in 70 age-related statistical chance of having a baby with Down Syndrome was about the same as my chance of winning a raffle prize at a school fete. And I never won raffle prizes.

To be honest, my emotional need to be pregnant that year was overwhelming. Maybe I would still have gone ahead even if the chance of Down Syndrome had been 1 in 2. I don't know. That afternoon I put the magazine aside and consoled myself with the assurance that it would be all right. It had to be. We had already had more than our fair share of bad luck. God wouldn't give me something I couldn't cope with. My baby was going to be just fine.

Our six children at Christmas 2006,
shortly before Martha was born

CHAPTER THREE: IS THERE A PROBLEM?

By the time the surgeon had finished stitching me back together after the c-section I had pretty much convinced myself there was nothing wrong. The doctors would have told me if there was a problem, wouldn't they?

I was wheeled into the recovery room where a midwife helped Adrian dress the baby in a nappy, vest and babygrow. No one mentioned anything about Down Syndrome, so I decided I must have imagined it. Brand new babies often look a bit funny, don't they? Maybe the anaesthetic medications had addled my brain.

Adrian passed Martha to me and I held her in my arms for the first time. I teased her cheek with my nipple, and after a little coaxing she opened her rosebud mouth and began to suck at my breast. Peace flooded through me as I cuddled my new child close.

Then it was time to go to the postnatal ward. I was soon settled in with my baby girl in her see-through hospital cot at my bedside. I struck up a conversation with the mum in the bed opposite and we were soon chatting about nappies, baby names and sleep (or lack of!). I felt happy and relaxed.

Adrian went home and came back later in the evening accompanied by some of the older children who were eager to see their new sister.

'Ah she's so cute!'

'I want to hold her!'

'Me now. It's my turn!'

There was quite a party atmosphere as we passed the baby around for hugs and kisses.

All my previous newborns had followed the same pattern on their first night. They had a good breastfeed shortly after birth and then slept for a good six hours or so. After that they woke up, screaming and ravenous, usually in the middle of the night.

Martha had only fed for a few minutes in the recovery room, so I fully expected her to wake hungry some time in the small hours. But when the sounds of the busy ward roused me at 6am I realised that she had slept all night without a feed. I picked her up and put her to my breast, but she was still sleepy and uninterested.

When a midwife appeared, I asked for her advice.

'My baby didn't wake all night for a feed. She's taken a little now, but is that something I should be concerned about? She's still very sleepy.'

The midwife hesitated for a moment.

'Well … some babies are sleepier than others. Especially after a c-section, sometimes. Try her again in an hour.'

Then she rushed away. Maybe she was just busy. But she didn't seem to want to meet my eye.

Once the day shift staff arrived I asked about my transfer to St Peter's, the little low-risk unit where I was planning my lazy convalescence. Maybe it was me, but again I sensed a hint of evasion.

'Well … let's wait and see shall we? Your baby needs to be checked over by the doctors first.'

The hours crawled by, as they do in hospital. I tried again to wake Martha for a feed and managed to persuade her to suck for a few minutes. At about 9am a young doctor arrived to do Martha's routine paediatric check-up. At least she said that's what it was. She listened to my baby's heart and inspected her spine and hips. She shone a torch into her eyes. Then she told me she needed to get her senior colleague to have a look.

'Why?', I asked. 'Is there a problem?'

'It's … it's her red eye reflex', she replied. 'I think I can see it, but I need to get the Registrar to check.'

I wasn't sure what red eye reflex was, but I didn't think it sounded too serious. At least she hadn't mentioned anything to do with Down Syndrome.

I prepared for another long wait, but the paediatric Registrar showed up at my bedside surprisingly quickly. She spent a long time looking at Martha. A worryingly long time. She didn't say what she was looking for, and I was afraid to ask. She looked carefully at the palms of both Martha's hands. That was when I began to feel afraid. I knew people with Down Syndrome had something different about the lines on their hands. But I was still scared to ask.

If nobody said it, it wouldn't be true.

'Is her red eye reflex ok?', I asked.

'Yes her red reflex is fine', she said. 'But she'll need to be seen by the Consultant Paediatrician. Is your partner coming in this morning?'

Adrian was due to visit at around ten. I had been hoping he would be ferrying me and Martha over to the little low-risk hospital. Now I wasn't so sure. I felt frightened and confused. Something was wrong with my baby, and no one would tell me what it was. The Registrar wouldn't say why we had to see the Consultant, and I couldn't bring myself to ask.

If nobody said it, it wouldn't be true.

My midwife wanted to know when Adrian was

coming. She seemed suddenly attentive, and she was being kind. Too kind. She asked me if I wanted a nice relaxing bath. Or could she get me a cup of tea? I shook my head.

'My husband will be here soon. I'll wait for him.'

Maybe they thought I was stupid. Maybe they thought I didn't care. I was sure they were talking about me and Martha in the ward office. But nobody would tell me what they were saying about my baby.

By the time Adrian showed up I was really frightened.

'They think there's something wrong with the baby. I think it's Down Syndrome. The doctor was looking at her hands. The palms of her hands. But no one is saying anything. We have to go and see the Consultant.'

Apparently the Consultant was too busy or important to come to the Postnatal ward. Accompanied by the alarmingly friendly midwife, Adrian and I were escorted downstairs in the lift to the Neonatal ward on the ground floor. Martha came with us in her wheeled cot.

'You're so lucky to be seeing Dr Shah*', babbled the midwife. 'He's such a lovely doctor. My little one has problems too, and Dr Shah has been marvellous with him.'

I know she was trying to be nice, but right at that moment I didn't want to know about the midwife's child. I didn't feel lucky, and I didn't care how lovely Dr Shah might be. I was nowhere near any sort of acceptance that our own baby might have 'problems', whatever that might mean.

Down on the Neonatal ward the midwife disappeared. Adrian and I were left standing in a corridor with Martha in her cot. After a few minutes a nurse appeared.

'Ok', she announced. 'So we're going to put a tube down your baby.'

''Er…. Why?', we both exclaimed in unison.

The nurse went away, and came back a few moments later.

'Oh I'm sorry', she said. 'We got you mixed up with another family. Your baby's here to be seen by Dr Shah. I'll take you into the parents' lounge, and he'll meet you in there when he's ready.'

Thoroughly shaken, we sat in the empty lounge. Neither of us spoke. We just sat and waited. It was probably only two or three minutes, but it felt like forever.

When Dr Shah arrived, he examined our baby carefully. He listened to her heart. He measured her head circumference, looked at her hands and her feet. Then, at last, he spoke:

'Ok', he said. 'We have some concerns about your baby. We need to do some blood tests to be sure. But I think it is probable, although not certain, that she has

Down Syndrome.'

The doctor had said it.

We had a problem.

* I have changed the name of the doctor to protect his privacy. I should add that he did in fact later turn out to be excellent, kind, and very helpful. But I did not know that at this point.

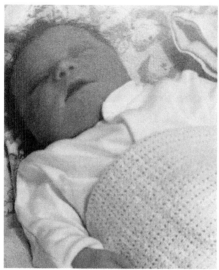

Martha sleeping

CHAPTER FOUR: A NARROW ROOM

Dr Shah said he needed to check Martha's heart, there and then. He spent some minutes scanning with a portable machine. There might be a couple of small defects, he told us, but it was too early to tell their severity. Often these things resolve on their own. He would make a referral for her to be seen by a cardiologist.

Then he gave us a booklet about Down Syndrome and said he would ask someone to take Martha's blood for a chromosome test. He also mentioned something that sounded like a Fish test. Apparently that would give us a quicker indication whether or not Martha had Down Syndrome, but it was less accurate than the full chromosome test. Or something like that. I was struggling to grasp information.[3]

When he asked if we had any questions, all we wanted to know was how quickly we could get the blood tests done. We just needed to know. One way or the other. Nothing else made much sense.

My baby screamed as the nurse took several attempts to draw blood from her tiny veins.

'I'm so sorry', said the nurse. 'We need quite a lot of blood for these tests.'

'Please try again', was all I could say. I didn't care that my baby was hurting. My need for an answer obliterated compassion.

Back on the Postnatal ward, the too-nice midwife closed the curtains round my bed. She brought me my lunch.

'There's apple crumble for pudding, but I don't suppose you'll feel much like eating right now?'

Hospital food wasn't up to much, but I liked apple crumble.

'Yes, I'll have that please.'

I felt absurdly angry. It was bad enough that my baby had Down Syndrome. Now they were trying to do me out of my pudding as well! The mind attaches emotion to the small things it can grasp.

Adrian and I exchanged practicalities. He needed to get home to the children. We would tell our mothers, but no one else until we had the test results. Dr Shah had said he wasn't certain, so there was still space for hope. But as Adrian was about to leave, he asked me if I was all right. I looked down at the sleeping baby in the cot. Tears pricked my eyes for the first time.

'No. Of course I'm not all right. You're leaving me here on my own. And I've got this … this defective baby.'

I was shocked by the bitterness in my voice.

I was told I couldn't go to the low-risk hospital now. They offered me a private room here in the main hospital instead. It was a narrow white room with a window overlooking the car park. It felt like a prison cell.

I sat alone in the white bed, Martha sleeping in her cot at my side. For long hours I had no one to talk to. The hospital staff were busy, Adrian was looking after the other children at home, and I didn't want friends to visit. I wouldn't have known what to tell them.

Rationally I knew the midwives had given me this single space as a kindness, but I felt as if I had been removed to avoid contaminating the other, normal mothers and their babies. When I left my isolation to make a cup of tea in the patients' lounge, I saw the mother I had been chatting with only last night. She didn't speak to me, and I didn't acknowledge her. I thought she might be afraid of me. She must know there was something wrong with my baby. I carried the miasma of bad luck about me. I was the bogeywoman now.

I cried in that little room. I cried a lot. Someone seemed to have turned on taps inside my eyes and the tears just wouldn't stop. I ate my chocolates and read my magazines, but nothing made me feel better. When my mother brought Verity and Jerome to see their new sister, I washed my face and smiled and pretended everything was all right. But it wasn't. Nothing was right at all.

I read the booklet about Down Syndrome over and over until I knew it off by heart. These were the days before you could easily google information on your mobile phone, so at least I wasn't tormented by an endless search for online answers. I spent ages gazing at Martha, trying to determine from the shape of her ears, her eyes, her fingers whether she really had Down Syndrome. The longer I looked, the less I knew. The not knowing was intolerable.

Sometimes I tested out accepting it. Ok, I told myself, so she has Down Syndrome. You know the doctor wouldn't have said so if he didn't think it was true. But I couldn't allow myself to believe it for long. If it was true, then my life was over. If it was true today, it would be true for the rest of my life. Until I died I would be the parent of a person with Down Syndrome. I didn't know how exactly, but I was certain my whole life would be blighted. This wasn't like an illness that might get better; this was no temporary setback. There would be no escaping it, no choice, no exit.

I was worried about Adrian. He hadn't even wanted a seventh baby, and now I had burdened him with a disabled child. When he came on his own to visit me I asked him:

'Do you think we should give up the baby for adoption?'

I was holding Martha close as I said it. I couldn't bear the thought of giving her away. I loved her. But I couldn't imagine us living the rest of our lives with her either.

'No of course not', he said. 'She's ours. We have to keep her.'

But he was grim-faced as he said it, and I wasn't sure whether to be sorry or relieved.

I asked for a hospital chaplain to come and see me. Maybe God had some answers. At least it would be a relief to speak with someone different. I was expecting a priest in black, but instead an elderly lady in a cardigan showed up.

'Hello', she said. 'I'm one of the chaplaincy team. Congratulations on the birth of your beautiful baby.'

She peered into the cot, smiling and cooing. She gave me a printed card with pictures of baby ducklings and Bible verses on it. She didn't say anything about Down Syndrome, and I thought the staff must have neglected to tell her.

'Thank you', I said. 'But, but ... they say there's something wrong with my baby.'

And then it all came tumbling out. I was telling this woman, this kind stranger, all about our terrible year. How Adrian's Dad had died so suddenly, and then my Dad too, and how this baby had been born on the exact anniversary of Adrian's Dad's death. And how I had been so sure, so certain, that God would give us something good after all the bad stuff. And how the baby was meant to be the good thing. But now, but now ....

As I dissolved into tears the chaplain held my hand. Then she spoke quietly but with conviction:

'But this wonderful baby *is* the good thing. Of course she is. You just can't see it yet.'

I was certain she was wrong. But her words stayed with me nonetheless.

Verity, aged three, came to visit me and Martha in the hospital

CHAPTER FIVE: THE PHONE CALL

The phone call came on a stormy afternoon. It was dark outside, a proper winter's day, but cosy enough in my kitchen. Baby Martha was lolling in her bouncy chair and I was cooking dinner for the family.

I had felt better since coming home. After three days in the hospital it was apparent that the blood test results might not arrive for a while yet, and my c-section wound was healing well. Indeed I had virtually forgotten I had had surgery; Martha's possible diagnosis consumed all my capacity for concern.

We pretended so hard that everything was normal that I almost convinced myself. Martha breastfed regularly, slept and produced dirty nappies like any other baby. Maybe her facial features were a little on the small side, the back of her head a bit flat perhaps, but in every other way she seemed just fine. My busy life of mothering filled my days, and home felt safe and ordinary. By the time the phone call came I was certain the doctors had got it wrong.

'Hello. This is Dr Shah from the hospital. Is that Mrs

Lawrence?'

'Yes. It's me.'

He is going to tell me it was all a mistake. We can celebrate this evening. I'll send Adrian out for champagne.

'Mrs Lawrence, I'm sorry but the FISH test results have come back positive for Down Syndrome. I'm afraid your baby does have Down Syndrome.'

'Are you sure? No. I don't think so. I think that must be wrong. You see, she looks so normal.'

'I'm sorry Mrs Lawrence, but there is no mistake. We will get the full chromosome results in another week or two. But this test is certain. I'm sorry.'

I put the phone down, my hand shaking. I was furious with Dr Shah. How dare he tell me such a thing and spoil my perfect baby? How dare he bring me this bad news? But even while a large part of my brain remained firmly in denial, I knew that, outwardly at least, we were going to have to acknowledge this news as true. We would have to start telling people Martha had Down Syndrome.

We began with our own children. We gathered them in the kitchen that evening, and Adrian told them their sister had a medical condition. As our children ranged in age from seventeen down to three it was difficult to get it right for all of them. We stressed that Martha wasn't actually unwell, although we were still waiting for some more tests on her heart. It would probably be more difficult for her to learn things. She might take longer than other babies to walk and talk. She was unlikely to do A levels or go to university.

Some of the older ones commented later that they had trouble calibrating the seriousness of what we told them. On the one hand we had presented this as a big family announcement, and we were clearly upset. Indeed Matilda, the eldest, said she had already known that there was something wrong from all the murmured conversations behind closed doors, and our anxious faces.

But then the symptoms we had described sounded pretty trivial. Was it all a big fuss about nothing then? I think I was experiencing some of the same difficulties myself. How could this contented and healthy-looking baby have such a huge shadow hanging over her future?

Adrian bought books: his go-to approach for all life's problems. For the younger children we purchased story books with pictures of happy families playing with their siblings with Down Syndrome. For ourselves we ordered a selection of informative books for parents, travel guides to the new territory in which we so unwillingly found ourselves. I spent many hours breastfeeding Martha in the rocking chair with one of these books in my hand, educating myself about poor muscle tone, developmental milestones and the importance of early intervention.

I found I could only tolerate a chapter or so at a time before the avalanche of information reduced me to tears. One of the difficulties of parenting a child with Downs, especially in the early weeks and months, is the vast uncertainty about how your baby might turn out.

The list of possible problems associated with Down Syndrome is long and terrifying. Your baby might have feeding problems, serious heart defects, respiratory illness, poor vision, hearing loss, thyroid deficiencies, spinal instability, missing teeth, seizures or leukaemia. Or she might have only a few or none of these health challenges.

As she grows, her physical and intellectual development will certainly be delayed, but this could turn out to be anything from fairly minor impairment to profound and devastating disability. As she ages, she may succumb to early-onset dementia. Or she may continue to live a full and active life until the age of sixty or beyond. Looking at the tiny baby in my arms, there was really no way of knowing. Yes, I had a diagnosis telling me she had an extra chromosome, but in many ways I was little the wiser as to how that third chromosome 21 would affect her life. Or mine.

All the books were agreed that educational and therapeutic interventions were essential, and from as early an age as possible. I have a responsible, proactive personality. When electronic 'pets' first came on the market, one of my children acquired this little gadget called a Tamagotchi that beeped for frequent attention. I used to interrupt my day to 'feed' and 'exercise' this pixilated thing while its owner was at school because I couldn't bear to think of it falling ill or dying from neglect. That's the kind of mother I am! So all the exhortations to stimulate and educate my impaired baby fell on hypervigilant ears. I was not going to make this easy for myself.

I contacted the Down's Syndrome Association (DSA)[4] as well as a local support group.[5] I felt sure there was something, probably lots of things, I should be doing, and I wanted someone to tell me what they were. I must have sounded on the phone as if I had my act together, because I remember the woman from the DSA saying to me,

'You sound as if you're coping well. But it's ok not be be ok, you know? It's still very early days.'

'I feel fine at the moment', I told her.

That was true, but half an hour later I was crying again.

The local support group sent me some back copies of their newsletter. These were full of black and white photos of older children and teenagers with Down Syndrome. They all looked happy, and I'm sure their parents thought they looked adorable, but I was horrified to think my baby might grow up to look like that. Flat-faced, heavy-built, squat, obviously mentally disabled - surely no one looking like that could ever be part of *my* perfect family?

I felt ashamed to have these thoughts. Surely now I was a Down Syndrome parent myself I shouldn't feel such prejudice? But it was rooted deep inside me, in a dark place I had never had to venture before.

CHAPTER SIX: DARK PLACES

I went to some dark places in those early weeks.

Outwardly everything looked fine. I cared for my new baby and my six other children with my usual efficiency. Everyone got to school or nursery on time. Everyone was neat and tidy, their clothes washed and ironed, hair brushed, teeth cleaned. Breakfasts were eaten, packed lunches made, and there was a home-cooked meal for the family each evening. The house sparkled and shone. The baby was fed, changed, cuddled and kissed. I did all the things I knew how to do so well. But under this shell of competence my mind and emotions were in chaos.

I was fortunate to have a lovely and caring health visitor[6] who came to see me and Martha at home once a week for the first couple of months. She used to weigh and measure Martha, ask me how I was feeling and make time for a quick chat. Usually I told her I was ok. But one morning I could no longer hold in my misery. While Martha lay on her colourful blanket on my spotless kitchen floor, my words went wobbly.

'It's just that … everything's just so rubbish all the time. I feel so, so … horrible.'

I sat down at the table in tears. She didn't say anything. She just held my hand. She held my hand while I cried, and I will be forever grateful for her kindness. Never underestimate how those small acts of compassion can make a difference. I will remember her hand holding mine for the rest of my life.

I told the health visitor I kept thinking about giving up my baby for adoption. Despite Adrian's assertion that Martha was ours to keep, and despite my own strong maternal love for my child, I couldn't let go of this idea that maybe we should give her away. It was because I felt trapped. Down Syndrome seemed like a black chasm that I had blundered into by mistake. I had to find a way out. I couldn't accept it.

'Do you *want* to give her up?', asked the health visitor doubtfully.

'No. Not really. I don't. I love her. But I'm worried about my husband, my family…'

Martha made a little sound and I gathered her up in my arms.
'You handle her so very lovingly', commented the health visitor. 'I can see that you care for her deeply. Why don't you talk to your husband about it?'

I didn't want to give Martha away. It would have broken my heart. But the thought kept returning.

There was something worse too. Something I didn't talk about to anyone. Sometimes I thought about killing her.

I don't think I would ever have acted on these thoughts, but I had a recurring fantasy of smothering her with a pillow. Martha was tiny and weak, and I knew, physically, it would be easy enough to do. In my lowest moments, when I was alone in the house with Martha, I imagined doing it. Obliterating my problem.

I was a Christian and a Catholic. I had always declined antenatal screening for Down Syndrome in all my pregnancies because I had been certain I would never want an abortion. And yet here I was thinking about murdering my living, breathing child.

I very much doubt I could have done it; my cornered mind was searching for any and every possible escape route like a rat in a trap. I remember thinking that I would very likely go to prison if I killed my baby. But that didn't feel like much of a deterrent. Emotionally, irrationally, the prison in my fantasy didn't compare with the prison I believed I was already inhabiting.

Probably the biggest protective factor was my profound commitment to my six other children. I might not mind about going to prison for myself, but I could not contemplate depriving them of my care. And when I thought about the adoption idea, I knew I could never,

ever tell my other children that I had given Martha away because there was something wrong with her. What would that do to them and their sense of security? It was unthinkable. Impossible.

I genuinely loved Martha. I breastfed her and sang to her and rocked her to sleep in my arms. I kissed her and caressed her tiny feet. I bathed and changed and dressed her with tender care. I researched her condition and sought out the best help I could find. I kept every medical appointment and worried over her weight gain. And I told no one at all about my darkest, most terrible thoughts. They might have taken her away from me, and that would have been unbearable.

Bizarrely, thinking about giving Martha away led me to one of my first emotional coping strategies. Even as I contemplated offering her up for adoption, I realised that I was exactly the sort of person who might choose to adopt a baby with Down Syndrome. In fact, if I had adopted her, I would actually feel rather good about myself, instead of this all-encompassing sense of failure. In other words, the problem wasn't that she had Down Syndrome; it was that I had given birth to her.

This was a revelation. Rationally I knew that Down Syndrome is a chromosomal condition that happens unpredictably and by accident. But despite this knowledge I felt terrible guilt that my body had brought a damaged child into the world. My mind repeatedly ran back over my pregnancy: that time I ate seafood, going for a long walk on a hot day, the time I fell down the stairs. I had to keep reminding myself that Down Syndrome was determined at the moment of conception; nothing I did while pregnant would have made any difference at all.

But the mind seeks reasons. And sometimes we have to play tricks with our minds, just to keep them quiet. So sometimes I pretended to myself that I had adopted Martha. I was not a defective mother of a broken baby. I was a noble and generous person who had chosen to take on a disabled child. It wasn't true, of course, but it helped me.

I was also helped very much by an older friend who had a mentally disabled son. This woman understood what I was going through. She had been there.

'I never thought it would happen to me', I told her. 'And I feel so guilty about that. Why did I think everything would be all right with my baby?'

'Of course you thought your baby would be all right', she replied. 'We all do. We are hard-wired to think that. How else would the human race continue?'

I took great comfort from those words. It was not my fault. My antenatal optimism was normal, not culpable. I needed to hear that.

And as the weeks rolled by, slowly, and with the help of good people, my mood began to lift a little.

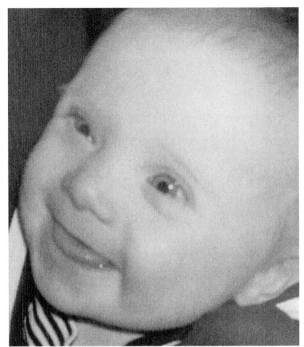

One of Martha's first real smiles

CHAPTER SEVEN: TELLING PEOPLE

Telling people about Martha was difficult. I felt acutely that I was at the same time imparting good news - 'we have a new baby girl' - and bad news - 'but she has Down Syndrome'. How was anyone supposed to react to that? I couldn't even work out how to react myself.

People's responses varied. Some acted as if they hadn't even heard the Down Syndrome bit, as if there wasn't a problem at all. That made me feel as if they thought this was easy, trivialising my grief. Others piled on the sympathy until I felt guilty. After all, most of the problems so far had been inside my head. Maybe I really was making a fuss about nothing very much.

To their credit, almost everyone congratulated me on my beautiful baby. But was she really beautiful, or were they just being kind? I had spent so much time staring at Martha's features, trying to work out whether or not she really had Down Syndrome, that I honestly had no idea. Until I saw a baby who didn't have Down Syndrome. Then the difference was obvious.

I found it very difficult to be around other babies

of a similar age. When I saw their big eyes and high, rounded foreheads I made instant comparisons with my own small and sub-standard looking infant. Other people's babies were more solid, more reactive, lively and smiley. I assumed those other mothers felt sorry for me, even though they never said so. Although I had six healthy older children of my own, I burned with unspoken jealousy towards these other parents with their normal babies. How dare they take their fat, alert bundles of joy for granted?

Other babies were everywhere, mocking me with their robust health and their rapid development. When I went to church there always seemed to be a baby in the next pew, wide-eyed and cooing. I queued up to receive holy communion behind families trailing sturdy toddlers and hefting huge infants. I swallowed what was supposed to be the bread of life with bitterness and sorrow in my heart.

I remember exploding with anger months later when we received a Christmas letter from my sister-in-law. Martha's cousin was just a few months older, and her mother wrote with cheerful maternal pride:

'She never seems to stop talking these days. We are amazed that she has learned so many words so quickly.'

I swore, loudly and furiously. Then I ripped the letter in half and stuffed the pieces in the bin. Martha, eleven months old by now, seemed unlikely to speak for years, if ever.

On another occasion I took Martha to a toddler group. Two mothers were comparing notes, as mothers do, fretting aloud that their babies, both aged around a year, were not yet walking independently. I felt irrationally angry that they should be having this conversation within my earshot. Didn't they realise my baby wouldn't walk until maybe age three, or even later? How could they be so insensitive? Struggling to hide my emotion, I went home early. I didn't go back to that group again.

When my other children were small, I had enjoyed taking them to various baby and toddler gatherings at local church halls or in the homes of friends. It had been a welcome opportunity for me to socialise and drink coffee with other mums while our little ones rolled around and played with toys on the floor. Mothers need other mothers, and I was no exception.

But with Martha I found I couldn't cope with these groups. No one ever said anything unkind or turned me away, but I knew I didn't belong. I hated the awkwardness of telling other mums that my baby had Down Syndrome. But equally I couldn't bear wondering what they were thinking about my slow, undersized child if I didn't say anything. Just like in the hospital, I felt as if I somehow cast a shadow over the other happy parents. I was a jinx, a blight, an unwelcome reminder of how close we all sail to disaster. No one ever suggested such a thing, but I felt it deep in my gut: mine was a cursed child, a primeval shame.

The obvious alternative was to seek out other parents of disabled children. This is where the local support groups came into their own. I was put in touch with other parents of children with Down Syndrome. It was helpful to compare notes and hear other families' stories, although this could sometimes be an emotional minefield too.

Inevitably, the other parents were all carrying stresses and anxieties of their own. And hearing about their children's progress, or lack of it, could be challenging. I tried not to look shocked when someone told me her twelve-year-old son had only just learned to write his own name. This was a reality check I wasn't ready to deal with.

And sometimes their children seemed to be doing better than mine. If it was difficult comparing Martha with normally developing babies, it was far worse seeing another child with Down Syndrome of a similar age who seemed to be streets ahead of her.

People with Down Syndrome, like all people, have a wide spectrum of personal strengths and weaknesses. Another child might walk much earlier than mine, but be much later to start talking, for example. But in these early, hyper-sensitive days I was easily distressed by any suggestion that Martha might be falling behind even her Down Syndrome peers.

I discovered that, just as you might expect, the parents of children with Down Syndrome are a diverse group of people. Just because someone has a child of a similar age with the same genetic condition, this does not necessarily mean she will become my new best friend. We might turn out to have other things in common and get on like a house on fire. Or we might not. Some of these contacts fell naturally into the background of my life. But over time I have made a few wonderful friends with disabled children. These people who genuinely 'get it' are a great support. I am deeply grateful for their enduring friendship.

I was hugely helped by a local centre providing support, information and activities for the families of children with special needs. SNAP[7] in Brentwood was a lifeline. At its bright and airy premises, we discovered regular groups for children and parents, beautiful toys, a chilled-out sensory room, a library, support for siblings, helpful advice, and friendly staff and volunteers always ready to offer a cup of tea and a listening ear. I started to go there at least twice a week, finding it to be a safe space where I felt accepted with my funny baby.

A friend who has a child with Down Syndrome de-scribes this experience as 'finding our people'. To begin with, meeting other parents of disabled children felt very much like joining a club I had never wanted to belong to. But it was such a relief not to be the odd one out here. Singing 'Old MacDonald had a Farm' with the others, and watching Martha enjoy the colourful light-up rattles, I smiled and began to relax. Maybe things weren't going to be quite so bad.

At SNAP I also began to become aware of other children with special needs and the huge pressures on their parents. Some children didn't obviously appear to have much wrong with them, or at least not until you witnessed their behavioural problems. Others had heart-breakingly profound disabilities, or life-limiting conditions.

My dark cloud of self-pity began to lift a little as I realised that Martha's problems were actually quite minor compared to the challenges faced by many of the other children. Here was a whole world of sorrow and courage, tragedy and positivity. I had never had to engage with it before. Now it got me thinking and asking questions. Lots of questions.

CHAPTER EIGHT: THE CHANGELING AND THE MOON

A changeling is a fairy, troll or elf left in a cradle in place of a human infant stolen by the fairies. The alien creature exchanged for the lost baby has a deformed appearance or strange powers. Often the changeling child is abandoned, abused, or drowned. Medieval European culture is full of tales like this

I had come across these legends decades ago, while studying for my degree in English literature. Considering myself to be a sophisticated modern person, I had dismissed such stories as superstitious nonsense. But after having Martha, the idea of the changeling came back to me. Now it had a new resonance.

As I have mentioned, imagining that I had adopted my strange-looking baby was a useful coping strategy in those early weeks. This is not so very different from the idea of the changeling: this infant is not mine. The perfect baby I had expected has somehow been stolen from me. I have been left in its place with something I am struggling to accept.

Maybe this sense of distance is a necessary part of the journey. Before I could wholeheartedly accept the damaged child in my arms, I had to grieve the loss of the perfect one in my imagination.

Visceral shame at bringing a disabled child into the world lurks deep in our cultural psyche. This is something we struggle to admit nowadays. I was unable to tell anybody about my dark thoughts of smothering Martha. But I suspect these impulses came from a powerful collective undercurrent that few of us can own up to.

Pretending that the different child is not human may have provided a justification for the practice of infanticide in earlier times. It is undeniably true that children with disabilities, even when greatly loved, can place a strain on the resources of both their families and the wider society. Even today UK law allows termination of pregnancy up until birth where the baby is expected to have a disability such as Down Syndrome. At the time of writing, this controversial provision is being challenged as discriminatory in the English courts by a young woman with Down Syndrome. [8]

These are uncomfortable issues. A detailed discussion is outside the scope of this book, which is intended to focus on my personal experience. But I would encourage you to give these difficult questions some careful consideration.

Asking 'Why?' when things do not go as expected is

a natural human response. It is one of our great strengths, fundamental to science, learning and discovery. But sometimes we cannot find easy answers. We know nowadays that children with Down Syndrome are not fairies or elves; they have an extra chromosome. But that does not explain the deeper question why such things happen at all.

I was brought up in a Christian family. As a teenager, I once asked my Dad how God could allow children to be born with disabilities. Surely that was completely unfair, when the children had done nothing to deserve it? My father said he thought God allowed this to teach people to be more compassionate as they cared for the weaker members of society. I disagreed. How could anyone justify the suffering of innocent children just for the sake of making other people kinder? And besides, not everyone treated disabled people well anyway.

Growing up, I retained my faith. I didn't really solve the problem I had posed to my Dad, but I dismissed it somewhere into the background. It didn't directly concern me anyway. If pushed, I might have fallen back on the argument that God only gives people the problems they are equipped to cope with. Without actually articulating it, I think I had a vague idea that Adrian and I, as a good Christian couple, were blessed by God with healthy children, almost as a reward. God was good. He was looking after us. Everything was fine. And besides, I was much too busy to worry about theoretical stuff like that.

So Martha's arrival was a huge reality check. Suddenly the questions came crowding in. Why had God allowed this to happen to me, to us? And why did other families have children destined never to walk or talk, to require devastating quantities of care, or to fade and die at an early age? Could I still trust God? Was he good? Did I even believe in him at all?

When faced with existential threat, our immediate response is usually fight, flight, or freeze. Where my Christian faith was concerned, I froze. I didn't stop believing, as such. I even carried on regular attendance at church and Bible study groups. But inwardly everything was on ice. I couldn't pray. Nothing made much sense. I suppose I just waited. I didn't know what else to do.

I rejected platitudes. There are plenty of them out there. Some well-meaning people like to tell you that God only gives special babies to special parents. I'm sorry, but I don't think so. I honestly did not believe (and still do not) that Adrian and I were particularly well equipped to care for a disabled child. And even if we were, many families are not, but still get disabled babies anyway. My more recent experiences as a midwife and health visitor have confirmed that, many times over. I have witnessed mothers tangibly unable to cope with the children they already have, pregnant again with severely damaged babies.

Some people tell you that you are lucky to have a child with Down Syndrome. You have been given an angel, a special gift from heaven. It is like winning the lottery, they say. Now this one is complex. Today, with hindsight, having traversed a lot of rough ground, I can honestly say that I believe Martha is one of the greatest blessings of my life. But that belief has been reached at a price. And a great deal of that price has been paid by Adrian, our other children and by Martha herself. I don't think anyone else has the right to tell you your disabled child is a special gift. At best it is something you can learn for yourself, painfully and over time.

Some people say there is no real problem. Children with Down Syndrome are just different, not worse. There is an oft-quoted poem, 'Welcome to Holland', which tells you having a disabled child is like going on holiday to Holland instead of Italy.[9] Someone will inevitably send you a copy if you give birth to a baby with Downs. But I feel this ducks the reality. Children with chromosomal disorders do have something *wrong* with them. It is a defect. People are not supposed to be born like this. And I had to face that fact and own it before I could begin to move beyond it.

That doesn't mean I think we should not care for people with disabilities to the utmost of our abilities. It doesn't mean their lives are not valuable, beautiful, priceless. It does not mean they do not have remarkable gifts for themselves and for others. But a disability is still a problem. Trying to pretend otherwise mocks the real day to day struggles and disadvantages faced by millions of people with disabilities and their carers. Don't tell me it's simply different. It is both more and less than that.

My faith remained frozen for much of Martha's first year. I will share more about that in later chapters. But I would like to close this one with a beautiful haiku by the seventeenth century Samurai poet, Mizuta Masahide. For me it incapsulates the way we have to experience real loss before we can begin to see any benefits:

Barn's burnt down.
Now
I can see the moon.

CHAPTER NINE: SHE'S NOT GROWING

During my pregnancy I had very much looked forward to breastfeeding one last baby. I loved breastfeeding all my babies. I loved the simplicity and the intimacy of that closest of all relationships. I relished watching each child grow and thrive on my milk. I couldn't wait to do it again.

As soon as I realised Martha might have Down Syndrome I was determined she would be breastfed too. I knew breastmilk helped support brain development and reduce the chance of various infections.[10] If any baby needed my milk, Martha did.

She had been sleepy and slow to feed for the first twenty-four hours or so. After moving me into my single hospital room, the midwife had asked if I would like to give Martha some formula milk.

'No thank you. I want to breastfeed her.'

'Are you sure? Usually babies like this…' She looked at me doubtfully. She didn't think we could do this.

'Could you get someone to bring me a baby bath with some warm water please? I think a bath might help her wake up.'

I undressed my tiny baby, bathed her and dried her. I kissed her and talked to her. Then I put her to my breast again. She opened her mouth and latched on with enthusiasm. After that I never had a problem persuading her to feed from me. It was a small and much-needed triumph.

In the middle of all the confusion and misery at that time, breastfeeding Martha was a constant comfort. I realise I was lucky. All my previous experience of feeding my six other babies was an enormous advantage. It had taken me several weeks of struggles and doubts to get the hang of breastfeeding my first child. If Martha had been my first baby I would probably not have had the confidence to persevere. No mother should feel bad if she is unable to breastfeed, for any reason whatsoever. But for Martha and me it was an oasis, a safe place, an island of normality in the stormy seas of that first year.

Martha slept beside me at night. She was always with me during the day. At the first snuffle or sign of movement I picked her up and fed her. Her little body was close beside me when I cried. She fed frequently and happily.

There was only one problem: she wasn't growing.

Martha's birth weight was a healthy 3.36kg, or 7 pounds 6 ounces, pretty good for a baby with Down Syndrome born two weeks before her due date. The Down Syndrome Association sent me some special centile charts for recording the growth of babies with Downs, so we used these to track her weekly weights and measurements.[11]

For the first four weeks she followed the fiftieth centile line exactly, indicating perfect average growth. The breastfeeding was working, and all seemed well. At around this time Martha had her follow-up appointment with Dr Shah. He did an echocardiogram[12] and confirmed that she had a small hole between the left and right chambers of her heart. He was hopeful that this might heal by itself over time and arranged for another scan a few weeks later. He did not seem too worried, so I did not worry much either. I was still overwhelmed by her Down Syndrome diagnosis and the heart business seemed unimportant by comparison.

In fact, I was still secretly hoping someone would tell me it had all been a mistake. Martha seemed so healthy, and my powers of denial were so strong that I was still a long way off accepting what we had been told. It felt like the story of the Sleeping Beauty, where the wicked witch casts a spell over a princess in her cradle, condemning a seemingly perfect child to a doomed future. Surely it couldn't be true? There had to be a magical solution. Perhaps none of the threatened disasters would ever actually happen. Perhaps the tests had got it wrong.

But over the next few weeks, Martha's growth began to stall. The health visitor did her best to reassure me, pointing out that Martha had increased in length, or was due a feed, or had just filled a nappy. But despite regular feeding my baby was gaining only a feeble fifty or a hundred grammes per week. And her weight was slowly but surely slipping down the centile lines on the chart. By four months she was down to the ninth centile. And she was looking scrawny.

At the next hospital clinic, Doctor Shah was joined by a cardiologist from London. The doctors listened to Martha's heart, repeated the echocardiogram, inspected the growth charts and watched her breathing. Then they told me there was a problem. A real problem.

Martha's heart defect had become symptomatic. The cardiologist pointed out to me how rapidly she was breathing, and the way her little belly sucked in under her ribs with every breath. He explained that the hole in her heart was now quite large. It was allowing oxygenated blood to leak from the left side of her heart into the right side. This meant Martha's heart had to beat harder and she needed to breathe faster and with more effort, just to stay alive. This was why she was not gaining weight; it was taking all her energy just to keep oxygenated blood circulating round her body.[13]

I was given diuretic medicines which I had to syringe-feed to Martha to reduce the load on her heart. I had to come back next week to see a dietician. Nasal tube feeding was mentioned. And Martha was going to need surgery. Open heart surgery to close the defect.

'When? How soon?' Suddenly I had so many questions.

'You'll need to take her to the Royal Brompton in London, to be seen at the clinic there. But we would like her to have the surgery within the next six weeks.'

'So, it's urgent then?'

'Yes, it's urgent.'

Suddenly my healthy baby with the vague curse hanging over her wasn't healthy any more. Now I had something real to worry about.

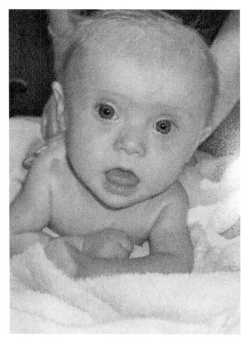

Aged four months, Martha was not
gaining weight

CHAPTER TEN: BLESSINGS, PRAYERS AND FEARS

Martha was going to have open heart surgery, probably within the next few weeks. We were told it was a relatively straightforward operation, but nevertheless there was a small risk of death or serious complications from the procedure. The doctors put this risk at between one and five percent. That might not have sounded too terrible, but I had recently faced similar odds of having a child with Down Syndrome. If we could be unlucky once, we could be unlucky again.

I tried asking what would happen if Martha didn't have the operation, but the doctors didn't really want to discuss that option.

'She needs to have this surgery', they told me firmly.

I did my own research online and learned that, without surgery, Martha faced increasing pulmonary hypertension, heart failure, failure to thrive, and death at an early age. There was no escaping it: she needed the surgery.

I decided I wanted her to be baptised as soon as reasonably possible. This wasn't quite as straightforward as it sounds. Adrian and I were both Christians, but while I was Catholic, he was Baptist. To complicate things even more, we had both been Baptist when we got married, but I had become Catholic some years later, at about the age of thirty.

The story behind my conversion to Catholicism could fill another book, so I will not attempt to explain it here. But our different church affiliations hadn't always been easy to negotiate, and we had had to work out some compromises. By the time Martha was born we were all attending the Baptist church together as a family, and I was also going to the Catholic church alone.

I was sad that none of my children had been baptised in the Catholic church which I saw as my spiritual home. I had prayed for many years that somehow things might shift in our rather uncomfortable church arrangements. But Adrian had been hurt by what he saw as my betrayal in becoming Catholic. It wasn't a subject we talked about much any more.

Now we had a baby with a life-threatening condition, facing surgery with an uncertain outcome. We had already arranged to have Martha dedicated in the Baptist church.[14] I asked Adrian if we could also have her baptised by the Catholic priest. He agreed at once. Like so many things with Martha, it was bitter-sweet. Here was the baptism I had dreamed of and prayed for. But it was happening because our child was damaged and in danger.

Why was Martha's baptism so important to me? I don't think I believed God would look on her with anything other than loving tenderness, baptised or not. But I wanted to give her every protection possible. I was completely unable to pray myself at this time. I couldn't even pray for Martha. But that was all the more reason for seeking the prayers and blessings of the wider faith community. She needed more help than I could give her on my own.

I have said that my faith was on ice at this time. I felt little or nothing when I attended church. Probably I was angry with God for giving me Martha, but I was afraid to explore those feelings. I didn't have the emotional headroom to indulge in such dangerous speculations. But I was mostly glad of the routine and the normality of churchgoing; it provided a safe space to be lost inside. The external frameworks of faith supported me, rather as a tree might support a weak and floppy plant beside it.

So we had two ceremonies of blessing: a dedication service at the Baptist church, and a Catholic baptism. Both were beautiful. At her Catholic baptism Martha had water poured over her head as the words of baptism were pronounced. Then she was anointed with holy oil, wrapped in a white shawl, and given a special candle. All this signified her new life in Christ. Despite her littleness and her vulnerability, she received the same gifts as anyone else.

For the Baptist dedication service, I chose a Bible reading which spoke to me of God's tender care for small and weak children like Martha:

At that time the disciples came to Jesus, saying, "Who is the greatest in the kingdom of heaven?" And calling to him a child, he put him in the midst of them, and said, "Truly, I say to you, unless you turn and become like children, you will never enter the kingdom of heaven. Whoever humbles himself like this child, he is the greatest in the kingdom of heaven. … See that you do not despise one of these little ones; for I tell you that in heaven their angels always behold the face of my Father who is in heaven. (Matthew 18:1-4, 10 RSV-CE)[15]

I think I wanted this passage read out in church to tell everyone not to despise my pathetic baby. But there was something else too. I needed to learn not to despise her myself. These words proclaimed that little, disabled children were powerful, the greatest, defended by front-ranking angels. I wasn't sure that I believed that yet. But I had an inkling that Martha had lessons to teach me.

We were moved by the concern and support of people in both our churches. Elderly ladies whose names I didn't know came up to me with gifts of toys and promises of prayers. They said Martha had touched their hearts. Sometimes I felt rather like the minder for a minor celebrity.

Our Baptist church even organised a special prayer meeting for Martha one evening shortly before her surgery. There must have been at least thirty or forty people, gathered just for us. I remember feeling grateful but embarrassed. I sat beside Adrian in the pew, head bowed, eyes closed, guiltily longing for it all to be over so we could go home. I had no idea whether all these prayers would make a difference. I knew everyone meant well. I knew they were being kind. I knew they believed. But I felt cold and empty inside.

How could I trust God? He had let Martha be born with Down Syndrome and with a hole in her heart. Who knew what else he might decide to do? I didn't dare address him, not even in silence. I was afraid his mysterious goodness was too alien, too dangerous. I never doubted that God loved Martha; I loved her myself, so that part was easy. But how that love might choose to express itself - who could say?

This year's journey had already proved so unpredictable. The ambivalence of my faith reflected my wider sense of travelling in uncharted seas. No longer in control of my own destiny, I was a passenger in a boat I couldn't steer. I had no idea where we were going next.

Martha on her Baptism day

CHAPTER ELEVEN: A SUMMER OF WAITING

It was a strange summer of waiting. We took Martha to the Royal Brompton Hospital in London where she was reviewed in their outpatient clinic. We were told we would get a date for her heart surgery within the next few weeks. We waited.

The doctors had stressed that the surgery was urgent, so every couple of weeks I phoned the hospital to ask if they had a date yet. Every time I was told it would be soon, probably within the next two or three weeks.

'Call us again at the end of this month', they said.

So I did. I kept calling, but the message was always the same. It will be soon. Soon, but not yet. The surgeon is on holiday. We need to be sure we will have an intensive care bed for her. We'll let you know as soon as we can. Yes, we understand it's urgent. Call us again soon.

The weeks turned into months. And we waited.

It was an anxious time. Martha was pale and breathless. Her weight crept along between the second and ninth centiles on her growth chart. But she smiled and played with toys. She became brighter and more responsive. She tried to roll over, and even sat up supported by lots of cushions.

I was feeding her butter now. Doctor Shah had told me bluntly,

'Your breast milk is not enough for this baby.'

It was a bitter blow, but the evidence was in front of me. The dietician reviewed Martha's charts and suggested NG tube feeding.[16] I was reluctant. I didn't want Martha to be discouraged from breastfeeding, and I hated the idea of more medicalisation. My baby looked different enough, without a tube taped to her cheek. I also worried that tube feeding would be very time-consuming. Family life with seven children was busy and demanding and I knew the other children needed my time and attention too.

Seeing my unhappy expression, the dietician came up with an alternative. Maybe I could try feeding Martha high calorie foods by mouth. Unsalted butter might work, and special high energy formula milk. But if that didn't work it would have to be a tube.

I mixed up thick pastes with butter, powdered baby

rice, fruit purees and the special milk. Martha was reluctant to drink from a bottle, so I spoon-fed her these calorific concoctions. We varied the flavour with different fruits and vegetables, and she seemed to eat it all happily enough. Fortunately, this strategy worked and Martha managed to gain just enough weight without the need for an NG tube. She carried on breastfeeding too, which reassured me. We had been told any infection could be serious, and I knew the antibodies in my milk were protective.

I gave her herbal mixtures as well. Back in the early weeks I had come across a theory that antioxidant herbal supplements, taken in large quantities, might possibly reduce the damage to the developing brain and nervous system in young children with Down Syndrome. I wasn't sure if I believed it, but I had to give it a try. How could I forgive myself if I missed a possible cure?

So for several months I purchased large tubs of a brownish gunk from an online supplier who assumed me all their herbs were grown organically and harvested at the full moon. Martha ate it all. By the following year the theory had been debunked by clinical trials.[17] I don't think the supplements did her any harm, but I was almost certainly wasting my money. I was desperate for a way out and searching hungrily for hope.

Even while I attended hospital appointments and worried over Martha's weight, I still fantasised about none of this being real. I remember one evening driving along a lane near our home and noticing a half-built new house surrounded by scaffolding. Somehow I convinced myself that the house had been fully built last time I had seen it, and that I had somehow travelled back in time. For several whole minutes I nearly believed this was true. I had miraculously gone back to the time before Martha was conceived. Now I could do things differently. All my problems had evaporated.

For much of Martha's first year I felt like two entirely separate people. There was the rational, intelligent woman, accepting reality, getting on with life, coping well with her vulnerable baby and her big family. She smiled, her house was clean, her children sat in a tidy row in church each Sunday.

And then there was the raving nutcase, this insane idiot who believed in time travel and magic herbs. The mad woman clutched at straws and refused to believe any of what they said about her baby. She still thought one day it would all turn out to be a big mistake. I did my best to bury that crazy me, but sometimes she popped up when I least expected her. Reality can take a surprisingly long time to digest.

One thing that really helped me in these months was baby massage. A friend had recently trained as a baby massage teacher, and she invited me and Martha along to her classes. Unlike some of the other babies who were reluctant to lie still for long, Martha adored being massaged. Calm and tactile, she lay back happily and let me rub her little feet, legs and belly with warm, oiled hands. I massaged her every day at home for months, and these intimate times together helped build the bonds between us.

Although she still showed no signs of developing speech sounds, Martha was becoming increasingly communicative in her own subtle ways. She was very aware of my moods, and I found her to be a loving and soothing presence. Touch was our main language, and it spoke volumes. In her smiles and her physical responsiveness, Martha was already demonstrating signs of the advanced emotional intelligence which characterises many people with Down Syndrome.

We had booked a holiday in France that summer, but I was too afraid of what might happen if Martha became unwell far from home. So we cancelled and arranged a short break at Center Parcs instead. Everything seemed normal enough as we splashed about in the swimming pool and the children rode bikes through the woods. Martha enjoyed sitting in the warm shallow water and playing with plastic ducks and watering cans.

But a shadow was hovering over us; the date for Martha's heart surgery had finally been set. The week after we returned home from holiday, we packed our bags for the Royal Brompton. The waiting was over.

Martha with her siblings at Center Parcs, shortly before her heart surgery

CHAPTER TWELVE: HEART SURGERY

Martha's heart surgery date was scheduled for Monday 4th September. It was not a date we would have chosen; our two sons, aged four and eleven, were both due to start new schools on that day. But choice was a luxury we didn't have.

My mother was planning to come to stay to look after the children while Adrian and I were at the hospital with Martha. But at the last minute Mum was unwell with a bad cold. She was willing to come anyway, but I was terrified she might bring some infection into the home to which Martha might succumb on her return. Instead, a wonderful friend from church offered to come in each day to help out.

The hospital wanted Martha there the day before the operation for some final tests. So on the Sunday we left our eighteen-year-old daughter in charge of her five siblings and set out for the Royal Brompton. I was sad to be missing my boys' first days at school, but all my focus was on my baby. As her brothers and sisters kissed her goodbye I was wondering if they would ever see her alive again.

The hospital provided simple but adequate sleeping accommodation for relatives of in-patients on its top floor. After a long day of echocardiograms, blood tests and x-rays we settled Martha in her cot on the children's ward and tried to get some rest ourselves. Our room was hot and stuffy. It was a relief to creep downstairs in my slippers and dressing gown to give Martha her midnight feed. Her body was soft and comforting against mine. I had never been separated from her for more than a few hours. Tomorrow I would hand her over into the care of strangers.

Our son Jerome had had a broken tooth extracted under general anaesthetic a couple of years previously when he was two years old. It was the simplest of procedures, but I will never forget the moment when the anaesthetist injected a white medication into a cannula in Jerome's little hand and my child flopped suddenly into unconsciousness. It was nothing like a natural falling asleep. It was as if he had died in front of me.

Now it was Martha's turn. I carried my baby down the long corridors to the operating suite. I talked to her calmly all the way. I smiled for her. I wouldn't let her see my fear. But the moment they injected whatever it was that made her eyes roll back in her head and her body collapse in my arms, I lost all composure.

'Let us take her now', someone said. 'We'll look after her.'

And then she was gone, and I was sobbing helplessly into Adrian's chest.

The operation would take four or five hours, they told us. Maybe longer. They would open my baby's chest and stop her heart. Then, while a heart-lung machine kept her alive, the surgeon would cut open her heart and sew a patch over the hole between her two ventricles. Possible complications included excessive bleeding, blood clots, infection, abnormal heart rhythm, heart block, and death. The surgeon had stressed that this was one of the more straightforward procedures he regularly performed. He was highly experienced, and the hospital was a centre of excellence for cardiac care.[18] But this was my baby, and I was afraid.

Adrian insisted that we go out while the surgery was happening. I felt it was my duty to sit in the hospital and worry, but my husband was doing his best to distract me. The medics had promised they would phone us once Martha was out of surgery, or if there was a serious problem. There was nothing we could do for her now. So we went out, my phone in my pocket like an unexploded bomb.

The Royal Brompton is in Chelsea, West London, in a smart area surrounded by cafes, restaurants and luxury shops. We drank coffee and ate pastries at a French-style patisserie. Then Adrian took me shopping for some new clothes. It felt surreal, as if we were acting in a play. Anyone watching us would have thought we were just another couple out enjoying a day of pleasant indulgence.

We sat down for lunch in a pizza restaurant. As the waiter was bringing my food, my phone buzzed. I snatched it up and pressed it to my ear, heart galloping. It was too soon. She couldn't be out of surgery yet. Something was wrong.

But it was only my mother, calling to let us know she was thinking of us.

'Mum', I gasped. 'I know you mean well. But please, *please* don't call me again until we let you know she's out of surgery. Please! OK?'

Eventually, hours later, the hospital called. The operation had gone well. Martha was out of theatre and was being stabilised. She would be going to the Paediatric Intensive Care Unit, or PICU for short. We could come and see her there soon.

I couldn't get back to the hospital quickly enough. We carried our shopping bags up to our little attic bedroom and then headed straight for the PICU. There we were told that Martha wasn't ready for us yet. We were taken to a windowless waiting room with a small sofa. There was a painting of a ship on the wall. We sat there for what felt like forever. How long could it take to stabilise a baby after surgery? The minutes rolled into hours. Perhaps there was a problem. I stared at the ship. It was tossing in stormy seas. This was taking much too long. Something must be wrong.

Finally someone came to call us.

'You can come and see her now.'

Martha was lying on her back on a cot, wearing nothing but a nappy. Wires and drains protruded from the bottom of her chest. She had a breathing tube connected to a ventilator taped to her mouth. Monitoring pads and lines and cannulas and blood pressure cuffs seemed to be attached to almost every part of her body. A dressing covered the long wound down the centre of her chest. She was entirely unconscious. But she was alive.

A cheerful Australian nurse welcomed us. She took time to tell us what all the different tubes and wires were for and explained the various numbers on the monitor screen. The plan was to keep Martha asleep and on the ventilator for the next couple of days or so. The pacing wires could be used to manage the rhythm of Martha's heart if it faltered.[19] Martha's condition was critical, but I realised she was in excellent hands. Her nurse's obvious expertise was matched only by the loving attention with which she tended to her little patient.

We spent some time sitting with Martha. I stroked her fingers and talked to her, although she didn't respond. I watched the coloured lines and numbers track her vital signs across the screen. When at last I left to take myself to bed, the nurse reassured me that I was welcome here at any time, day or night. I felt grateful and exhausted. We had survived the day.

CHAPTER THIRTEEN: HOSPITAL STAY

Martha's hospital stay was a strange time out of time. After the first couple of days Adrian split his time between the hospital and home with our other children. I remained in London with Martha.

In practical terms I had very little to do. All round the clock, a trained professional attended to my unconscious baby's every bodily need. An intensive care nurse turns out to be the ultimate childcare solution. For a mum of seven, used to being constantly busy from dawn until well after dusk, this was unsettling. It was a strange, enforced retreat, an uncomfortable holiday.

I sat at Martha's bedside, talking with her nurses, and watching her breathe. She was asleep for three days. I soothed her cracked lips with vaseline on a cotton swab. I learned to interpret the screen above her cot. Sometimes her heart rate was too fast, or her temperature too high. I worried when her vital signs crept outside the safe range. I knew the nurses were the experts, but shouldn't they be doing something now?

On the afternoon of the second day the lines on the screen suddenly went haywire. The machines started beeping urgently. Martha's nurse looked alarmed. She called out for help, and several other nurses all rushed over. The normally calm but watchful atmosphere in the PICU morphed into frantic action. All the parents were sent out of the room.

I stood helplessly in the corridor outside, afraid to breathe, afraid to think. None of the parents said anything. No one met anyone else's eye. But a few agonising minutes later we were all allowed back in. One of the tubes from Martha's ventilator had come loose, the nurse explained. It was all ok again now. It was just a scare. She was fine. The lines on Martha's monitor had resumed their steady pattern. But it took a long time for my own heart rate to recover.

Martha was being fed via the naso-gastric feeding tube we had avoided all these past months. She couldn't breastfeed for now, so I spent regular periods sitting in a little side room off the main children's ward, pumping my breasts to keep my milk supply going. The television was always on in this room, and I sat here for hours, day and night, attached to the pump while the screen flickered in front of me.

The news reports were still talking about Madeleine McCann, the blonde haired three-year-old who had gone missing earlier that summer.[20] The story wrung my heart. I could not imagine a worse experience than having a child disappear, her fate unknown. Even if Martha were to die, at least I would know what had happened. The agony of Madeleine's parents was unthinkable. Although I was still unable to pray for Martha or myself, I found myself praying for Madeleine's family now.

The world seemed full of parents in anguish. One evening, sitting in the family lounge at the hospital to eat my microwaved dinner, I got into conversation with another mother. Her eleven-year-old son had just been diagnosed with a rare form of lung cancer. She was beside herself with grief. Her boy was the same age as my eldest son who had just started his senior school. I felt a surge of empathy. With nothing else to offer her, I promised to pray for her child.

On the morning of the third day, the nurse was concerned. Martha's temperature was well outside the normal range, and they were worried she had an infection. She was being given antibiotics. Her oxygen saturations were lower than they would wish. Adrian was away at home that day, so I was on my own. I couldn't bear to sit and look at Martha for long, so I took myself off to breakfast at a nearby cafe. My chest ached with its leaden lump of fear.

As I sat over my coffee and croissant, my phone pinged with a message. It was from Matilda, our eldest daughter. A few weeks previously she had received her A level results. She had just missed securing her hoped-for place at Cambridge University by one percentage point on one exam. We had applied to have this paper re-marked. But now this morning Matilda had received bad news: her marks were unchanged, and Cambridge had eluded her.

In that whole week, this was my lowest point. I felt alone and completely helpless. I was a mother. I was supposed to care for my children. I couldn't help Martha, whose vital signs were all headed in the wrong directions. I couldn't be there to hug and comfort Matilda in her disappointment. I hadn't been there to see my two boys safely into their new schools. I couldn't even face calling Adrian. All I could do was sit here and cry into my coffee.

Eventually I roused myself enough to message a trusted friend. Her quick reply with promises of many people around the world praying for us lifted me a little. Then I returned across the road to the hospital. I would phone home later, when maybe I could trust myself to speak without tears.

But thankfully, from then on, Martha began to improve. The antibiotics did their job. Her breathing, heart rate and temperature all found their way back to normal. The next day she had her ventilator tube removed. Now she was breathing for herself, with some supplemental oxygen to begin with. I spent more time with her now. She was starting to wake up. She responded to my voice and my touch. My baby was coming back.

At last I was allowed to hold her. The nurse carefully sorted out the tubes and wires as she handed Martha into my arms. I held her close, warm and alive, so familiar and so good. The morning in the cafe had been the worst moment, but this was the best.

'Can I put her to my breast?', I asked. 'She's looking for it.'

'Well maybe just for a moment. But don't tire her out'

I offered Martha my nipple and she took it instantly. She sucked, long and slow and peaceful. She was where she belonged. We were together again.

From that point on, Martha progressed amazingly quickly. The various tubes and attachments came out one by one. She fed from me at regular intervals, longer and stronger every time. By the fifth day she was out of the PICU and onto a general children's ward. She started eating solid food again.

On the Saturday morning she pulled out her own NG feeding tube.

'She doesn't need another one, does she?', I asked.

'No, I don't think so', agreed the nurse. 'I think she's telling us she's better. We'll have to wait for the doctors, but I expect she'll be able to go home tomorrow.'

This time I couldn't wait to call Adrian and tell him the news. We were going home.

CHAPTER FOURTEEN: GROWING AND LEARNING

The speed of Martha's recovery was startling. On her last day in the hospital she amazed me by sitting up unsupported for the first time ever. By the time we brought her home she was smiley, alert and active, stronger already than the fragile baby we had taken for life-saving surgery only a week earlier. Apart from the long wound down the centre of her chest, she looked remarkably well.

And she was growing. After all those worried months when Martha's weight dragged along the bottom of the chart, now the numbers climbed steadily. She carried on with the high energy formula milk for a while, as well as breastfeeding and eating an ever more varied range of solid foods. Soon she was joining in with family meals, where she developed an annoying habit of throwing any food she disliked straight onto the floor.

Martha's doctors pronounced themselves happy

with the outcome of her surgery. Their echocardiogram showed a good result, but our newly vigorous baby was the real proof. Martha was here to stay.

I was relieved, but not euphoric. The huge burden of Martha's heart condition had been lifted. But another weight remained: she still had Down Syndrome. There was no operation for that.

Sometimes I found myself wondering if I would prefer to have a child with a terrible but curable condition like cancer, or one with a lifelong disability like Down Syndrome. It is a cruel and impossible comparison, but I couldn't stop playing these mind games with myself. Other parents of children with disabilities have told me they have had similar thoughts. It is the mind struggling to make sense of things. But of course, no one is given such a choice. How could you choose anyway?

Martha was nearly nine months old by now. She was stronger by the day, but falling behind other children in her development. She could just about sit up, but showed no signs of crawling. She didn't make speech sounds. She could pick up toys and throw them, but that was about it. All the books had told me that early and intensive intervention was crucial to help children with Down Syndrome learn to the best of their potential. It was time to get on with it.

And so we turned our full attention to the therapists. There were lots of them. Martha saw speech therapists, occupational therapists, specialist teachers, physiotherapists. I even started seeing a therapist myself, to help me process some of the emotional issues of the past months. Sometimes the therapists came to our house; sometimes we drove to clinics to see them. I was incredibly grateful for all this help. In other countries or other times Martha would not have received any of this input. But it was all quite exhausting too.

In between managing all the needs of the older children, doing the school and nursery runs, running the home and trying to keep our marriage going, I seemed to have become a full-time therapist myself. None of the speech therapists or OTs[21] or physios[22] had the time actually to work with Martha on a daily or weekly basis. Their role, I soon learned, was to assess Martha's needs and then prescribe a set of exercises or interventions for me to carry out with her at home. Ideally every day.

Soon I was rolling balls, blowing bubbles, laminating flashcards, and lining up plastic farm animals on a regular schedule. Plenty of the recommended activities were playful and often fun, but the programmes carried with them a burden of duty. I would have to report back to the therapist at the next visit on how well I had done. It was a pressure I had not experienced with any of my other children.

Sometimes Martha liked the educational games, engaging enthusiastically in shaking maracas and rolling balls through tubes. But on other occasions she treated my efforts with disdain. Trying to persuade her to drink out of a cup was a particular battle. I lost count of the number of beakers flung across the room. At least she was developing a good aim!

The occupational therapist arranged for Martha to have a special chair. More supportive than a standard highchair, it was designed to enable her to sit up in a good upright position to engage in learning games, as well as for mealtimes.

The chair was delivered one afternoon by a man in a delivery lorry. It was an ugly, unwieldy object, with a red tubular metal frame, definitely second-hand. Garish cartoon animals leered at me from its vinyl cushions. It looked horribly out of place in my farmhouse-style kitchen, an invader from planet disability. I knew I was supposed to feel grateful for it. I loathed it. When no one was looking, I kicked it and swore. Bad enough that I had a child with Down Syndrome. Now I had to have this revolting piece of trash in my nice house.

Later I wiped my tears, scrubbed every corner of the offending chair with my harshest household cleaners, and put on a positive smile. I had had my tantrum. Now I just had to get on with it.

Working with Martha at home could be demanding. It was easy to get discouraged on my own. Increasingly I started taking her along to groups where she could take part in helpful activities with other children, and I could get out of the house. We went regularly to the play and therapy sessions at SNAP, our brilliant local special needs centre. There we had fun with music, messy play, soft play and lots of specialist toys. I got the chance to chat with other parents here, and there was always a cup of tea and a chocolate biscuit too.

We also started attending several 'normal' baby and toddler classes where I felt Martha could benefit from the equipment and activities on offer. Tumble Tots gave her the chance to roll, and later bottom shuffle, around simple obstacle courses and to bounce on mini trampolines. She liked the singing at the beginning and end of these sessions too, and the leaders and other parents were particularly friendly.

We tried baby swimming classes, but these proved frustrating as Martha seemed frightened of the water and clung desperately to me. There was always a fine balance between stretching her horizons with new opportunities and feeling crushed by the comparison between her and the other babies. Those others seemed so much more agile and more confident than Martha, reminding me painfully of her difference. The swimming lessons ended in tears.

But then we discovered baby signing classes. I was aware that children with Down Syndrome were usually late learning to talk, and that speech could be an area of particular difficulty. I had also read that simple sign language was often helpful in helping these children communicate. So I took Martha along to a class designed to teach sign language to normally developing babies and their parents. She loved it. So did I. It was to open doors I could not yet imagine.

Martha rapidly gained weight and grew
stronger after her surgery

CHAPTER FIFTEEN: YOU ONLY HAVE TO LOVE THIS CHILD

Christmas was approaching fast. Martha would soon be one year old. Outwardly we were doing ok. Martha was robust and thriving now. We were enjoying a busy round of weekly classes and therapy sessions together. She laughed and ate solid food, and all her siblings adored her.

No longer did I consider giving Martha away; I loved her like part of myself. And gradually, over the course of many months, I had come to accept her diagnosis. I had stopped half expecting Doctor Shah to call and tell me it had all been a mistake. I knew in my heart that she had Down Syndrome, and that it wasn't going to go away. And I knew she belonged to us.

I still balked at pictures of teenagers and adults with Down Syndrome. It worried me that I still felt something akin to revulsion at their flat faces and heavyset bodies. I used to look through publications from the Down's Syndrome Association or our local support group, searching out the most 'normal' looking faces. Maybe it will be all right, I tried to reassure myself. Maybe Martha will turn out looking like that one. Please not like that one on the next page with the tiny eyes and the mouth lolling open.

But then one day I had a small breakthrough. It came to me as I was wiping food from Martha's sticky little face, kissing her cheeks as she giggled.

I only have to love my own child.
That is enough.

No one was asking me to look after all the children in the world with Down Syndrome. I didn't need to love them all. No one expected that of me. All I had to do, right here and now, was to love this one child with Down Syndrome, right here in front of me.

And that was easy.
I already loved her.

It felt like a revelation. The cloud of guilt that had smothered me for months began to soften a little. And after that moment, when I stopped trying too hard, the feelings of fear and distaste at other people with Down Syndrome went away. I had been imagining that my own child would somehow turn into a monster, when in fact she was simply herself. All those others were just themselves too. There was no huge burden on me to look after them. And actually, especially when you met them in the flesh, they were all beautiful in their own unique way.

There is something instantly recognisable about a

person with Down Syndrome. I knew the first moment I saw Martha. Our race memory, our remarkable ability to read human faces, knows the signs. It is hardly surprising that this stirs up strong emotions.

In the past people with visible disabilities might have been singled out for abuse or exclusion. I am delighted that UK law now protects people with disabilities from discrimination. Many times, we have relied on this to get Martha the support she needs. But I also believe it is important to be honest about our deep-rooted gut responses. Disability still makes many people feel uncomfortable.

A visible disability is both a blessing and a curse. Martha's physical appearance, combined with her diagnosis shortly after birth, has opened many doors. Specialist educational interventions, discounted tickets at tourist attractions and friendly smiles from strangers have all come our way. I will never forget the wonderful lady at the London Aquarium who took one look at Martha's face and sent us straight to the front of a heaving hour-long queue! We were lucky. Children with undiagnosed conditions, or those who appear 'normal' but behave otherwise, often experience much greater difficulty getting the help and understanding they deserve.

But on the flip side, people often make the unwarranted assumption that Down Syndrome is a blanket definition. There is a widespread view that people with Down Syndrome are essentially all the same. They can be viewed as another species, a bit like puppies or kittens.

'Ah they're so cute.'

'These children are angels.'

'They're always happy, aren't they?'

'Ooh a little Downs! You've got a little Downs! You're so lucky.'

In reality, people with Down Syndrome are as diverse as any other group of people. While they will have many of the particular physical traits which characterise Down Syndrome - the flattened facial profile, shorter fingers and eyes that slant upwards and outwards - people with Down Syndrome resemble other members of their own families more than they look like other people with Down Syndrome. The range of intellectual ability within the spectrum of people with Down Syndrome is as wide as that in the general population. And people with Down Syndrome experience the same hopes, desires, emotions and frustrations as anybody else.[23]

Martha has never been an angel. And she is not always happy. She can be infuriatingly stubborn, grumpy, miserable, and downright sulky. She pretends not to hear me if I make an inconvenient request. And her deviousness at getting her own way defies description. She is a unique individual. She is a human child, with her own complex web of strengths and weaknesses. She is herself. She is not, and never has been, 'a Downs'.[24]

I loved Martha, dearly and devotedly. But there was

still a bitterness inside me. As Christmas drew near, I thought about all those families I had encountered in the past year with broken, damaged children. I remembered them as we decorated the house for the coming festivities. We unpacked the nativity set I had hand-sewn years ago. Here were Mary and Joseph, and here was baby Jesus in his manger. Weren't they supposed to be the perfect family?

What would it have been like, I wondered, if Jesus had had Down Syndrome? Could God's special baby have been anything but perfect? I wasn't sure if it was blasphemous, but I imagined a stable scene where all the characters had those unmistakable marks of Down Syndrome on their faces. Mary, Joseph, the angels and shepherds, yes and even Jesus too, all with flat faces, little ears and slanted eyes. If I were an artist, I would have painted it. I wasn't sure why, but to me it was beautiful.[25]

I kept pondering this picture in my mind over those days. The face of a baby with Down Syndrome, and the human face of God. There was a mystery here. It felt as if a key was being fitted into a lock, somewhere deep inside me. In this season of gifts and new hope, something was being released.

CHAPTER SIXTEEN: CHRISTMAS CONFESSION

It was just a few days before Christmas. Like a good Catholic, I had come to the church to make my confession.[26] Coming in from the damp December gloom, I blessed myself with holy water and sat down in the pew to wait my turn.

There were plenty of people ahead of me in the queue, so I had time to think. I was supposed to think about my sins. What was keeping me from getting closer to God? What obstacles needed to be cleared away from my life? There were the usual swear words, flashes of anger and lapses of temper. But really there was just one thing: I couldn't forgive God for giving me Martha.

It was in church that I felt my anger most sharply. There were always other babies here to remind me that Martha was different. It didn't seem fair. Here were all these other families with children that looked as if they had no problems. Why had God singled out my child for a heart defect and lifelong mental disability?

In recent months I had begun to pray for other grieving parents. There was the mother whose little girl had just been diagnosed with Rett Syndrome, a cruel disorder where an apparently healthy baby regresses into severe disability.[27] I had met her at a local group, along with parents of children with cerebral palsy, autism, and a plethora of rare syndromes. There were other parents of children with Down Syndrome. There was the mother of the boy with lung cancer I had talked to at the Royal Brompton. And I still prayed for the parents of Madeleine McCann.

I felt an affinity with all these sorrowful mothers. I could not claim to understand their personal pain, but I knew what it felt like to hurt over a child. I prayed for them all, asking that somehow they might find the comfort, the strength they needed. But I still could not pray for myself or for Martha. I felt as if God had shut me out. Or perhaps I just didn't want to talk to him about it. He had done this to me and my family. He had put me through all this unhappiness. I was furious with him.

At last, my turn came and I sat in front of the priest in the little confessional room. He was a youngish priest, one I had never met before. I went through the usual preliminaries and mentioned a couple of minor failings. Then I said,

'Father, I have a baby with Down Syndrome. She's almost a year old. And, the thing is, I'm just so angry with God for giving her to me. I don't know what to do about it.'

He paused. He was silent for a long moment. Maybe he would tell me to pray more. Maybe he would prescribe extra Hail Marys, or an improving book to read. But instead, he said something I had not expected:

'Have you ever thanked God for this baby?'

It was a bold question. I might easily have been angry with the priest. I might have protested that this childless man had no right to challenge me like this. But his words went straight to my heart.

'No', I said, and as I spoke the word I realised it was true. 'No Father, I have never thanked God for her.'

'Go and do that now', he told me. 'Before you leave the church today, thank God for your child.'

Then he gave me God's forgiveness for all my sins and wished me a happy Christmas. There was no other penance. Nothing else was required of me.

I made my way to a quiet corner of the church where votive candles burned in front of a statue of Jesus. I knelt down. Then, not knowing whether or not I meant them, I whispered the words I had been given:

'Thank you, God. Thank you for giving me Martha. Thank you.'

As I spoke the words under my breath, the tears

began to flow. I covered my face with my hands, but the tears were running down between my fingers. My whole face was wet with them.

'Thank you', I repeated. 'Thank you. Thank you. Thank you.'

And the tears dripped down my nose and off my chin and kept on flowing.

'Thank you.'

I don't know how long I stayed there. I don't know if anyone saw me and wondered why I was crying in the church. But as I voiced my quiet thank yous for this most difficult of gifts, I knew they came from my heart.

Martha had brought me great sorrow, but she had brought other things too. She had opened my eyes to some of the griefs of other families. She had introduced me to wonderful people I would not otherwise have met. She had taught me to accept help from strangers. She had shown me how resilient a tiny person can be. She had softened my self-satisfaction and challenged my proud assumptions. She had loved me completely, and accepted my love in return. And she wasn't even one year old yet.

I thought back to those early days after Martha was born, when the old lady chaplain had visited us in the hospital. I had complained that I was expecting something good from God after all our losses. Instead I had received this damaged baby.

'But your baby *is* the good thing', the chaplain had told me.

I had been so certain she was wrong.

But today, almost a year on, I wondered if perhaps she was right after all.

When I left the church that day, something was different. I didn't feel bitter anymore. I never met that young priest again, but, whoever he was, I believe God gave him those words for me. Once I had thanked God for Martha, something was released inside me. My anger seemed to have dissolved away in my tears.

Martha and I and the family still had plenty of challenges ahead of us. It wouldn't always be easy. But I was prepared now to unwrap the gift I had received. I went home smiling that day, ready to celebrate Christmas with my family.

CHAPTER SEVENTEEN: COMMUNICATION AND CONFIDENCE

As Martha passed her first birthday and continued to grow, our focus was increasingly on her communication and development. Her health was generally good now. She had occasional heart check-ups where the doctors pronounced themselves delighted with the outcome of her surgery. She ate well, and, despite my best attempts to persuade her otherwise, lost all interest in breastfeeding by about fifteen months. I was sad to stop breastfeeding my last baby sooner than I had hoped, but Martha was just too interested in taking in the world around her.

Her hearing was a cause for concern. Children with Down Syndrome tend to have very narrow ear canals which easily block up with mucus, resulting in glue ear and hearing loss.[28] Since Martha was likely to be slow to learn to speak due to her learning disability, any hearing impairment was a big deal. So she went twice for surgery to insert grommets.[29]

Compared to her cardiac operation, grommets seemed pretty minor, so the first time round I went to the hospital with Martha on my own. Although the nurses were lovely, this was more demanding than I had blithely anticipated. Keeping a nil-by-mouth child happy and entertained on the morning before any operation is hard work. Then I got anxious because the procedure took longer than I had been told to expect. It is hard not to start imagining the worst when you are alone and your child is in theatre. In the end the procedure went fine, but I was a wreck by the time we finally returned home.

Eight months later, when more grommets were required, I had learned my lesson. This time I asked two friends to accompany me and Martha for her day surgery. The whole experience felt so much easier when I wasn't trying to do it all on my own. Slowly, and still with some reluctance, I was learning to ask for help when I needed it.

Most children with Down Syndrome have difficulty and delay in learning to talk. But they tend to understand much more than they can say. This was certainly true for Martha. One of the most positive activities we enjoyed together was simple sign language. Adrian and I attended a course for parents to learn Makaton. This is a language with signs and symbols designed to be used alongside speech for people with learning or communication disabilities.[30] We were thrilled when Martha first started waving hello and goodbye. Soon she added the signs for 'food', 'drink' and 'more' to her vocabulary. 'Biscuit' and 'cake' also became firm favourites. We were communicating!

The 'Sing and Sign' classes designed for babies and toddlers of all abilities were so much fun, and so helpful. Martha and I learned lots of songs with accompanying signs we could practice together at home. The teacher was kind and encouraging, and I felt that we belonged.

Later, when Martha was two years old and attending nursery, I trained to become a baby signing teacher myself. This became my first foray into the world of work since Martha was born. It gave me a new sense of freedom and identity. I loved welcoming parents and babies along to my classes. As well as many typically developing children, several toddlers and babies with special needs came along. We all enjoyed singing, dancing and learning to sign together. Some of those mums have become firm friends. I would never have got involved with any of this without Martha to show me the way.

Martha's regular round of therapists continued, but I gradually became less in awe of them. At the beginning I had believed that everything depended on the right therapy. Maybe if Martha had enough speech therapy, enough physio, if I did all the right activities with her every day, maybe her Down Syndrome would somehow go away. Or at least it might hardly be noticeable.

But as the months rolled on, and especially after that first Christmas, I began to accept Martha as she was. Yes, I wanted to get her all the support she needed to grow and learn. Yes, I still spent many hours encouraging her to interact and communicate. But I no longer had that desperate need to change her. She would always have

Down Syndrome. It was an aspect of who she was. And that was ok.

This growing acceptance had some surprising results. Now, if I didn't think a therapist's interventions were helping, I would say so. Politely of course! I even said no thank you to the offer of a specialist health visitor, and asked for a change of speech and language therapist on one occasion. Just because someone was sent to my home by the education or health authorities did not necessarily mean they had all the answers. Frequently the therapists were great, but not always.

All the therapies and interventions consumed a lot of time and energy, so they had to make a difference. I no longer felt obliged to make Martha do all the exercises and activities proposed. We did the ones that worked for us. Martha didn't belong to the speech therapist or the occupational therapist or the specialist teacher. She didn't even belong to the doctors. I was her mother, and I knew her better than anyone else.

It can take a long time to reach this realisation when your child needs a lot of medical and therapeutic input. Of course, all the professionals had a lot of invaluable input. We were extremely grateful for it. But Martha was part of our family. And we loved her exactly as she was. She was herself, and that was just fine.

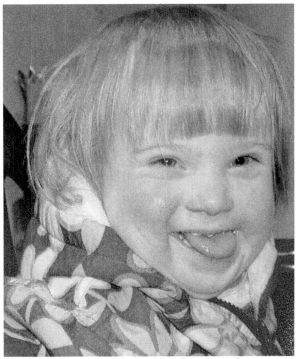

As Martha grew bigger she developed a great
sense of fun

CHAPTER EIGHTEEN: FAMILY IMPACT

Martha's six older siblings loved and accepted her from the start. That was never in question. So far as they were concerned, she was their baby sister; anything to do with Down Syndrome was insignificant by comparison. But her diagnosis inevitably had an impact on them. How could it not?

I am focusing on Martha in this book, but of course our other children continued to have their own worries and hopes, successes and sorrows. They needed my attention too. I did my best, but sometimes that attention was elsewhere.

When Martha was still only a couple of months old, our son Petrok broke his arm. Aged eleven, Petrok was away at a boarding school for children with dyslexia. Another child's roller-skate fell out of a high locker and landed on his wrist. He spent a whole night sleepless with pain before anyone took him seriously. I wanted to rush to Petrok's side, but the needs of my fragile baby, plus our two other pre-school children, left me paralysed and helpless. Someone else took Petrok to hospital; I wasn't there for him.

I have mentioned that our two sons, Petrok and Jerome, both started new schools on the day Martha had her heart surgery. To make matters worse, Petrok missed his bus stop on the way home from school that first day. We had to arrange for a friend to rescue him from the bus depot because we were too busy in London with Martha. It wasn't the best beginning, and Petrok found it difficult for some time to settle at the school. Once again, I didn't seem to be around when it mattered.

People often talk about how children benefit from having a sibling with special needs. These benefits are real, but they come at a price. All Martha's brothers and sisters are unstintingly kind, patient, caring and tolerant. I am proud of their gentle and unselfish characters, but I am also painfully aware that they had little choice about becoming young carers. Each of them has spent many hours playing with Martha, babysitting her, feeding her, reading her stories and tucking her into bed at night. Helga, aged ten at the time, used to help me with Martha's exercise routine every morning before school; she is now a nurse, caring for vulnerable young people. Sometimes I worry that she cares too much.

It is well documented that the siblings of children with special needs have increased risks to their psychological and educational wellbeing.[31] A great deal is asked of them. I am incredibly grateful that Martha has six loving older brothers and sisters. Martha adores them all, and their input has made my life immeasurably easier. Looking to the future, I take huge comfort in the knowledge that Martha has these wonderful siblings to look out for her when Adrian and I may no longer be able to do so. It must be incredibly tough to have an only child with a disability. But I do worry about the additional demands on Martha's siblings. It seems unfair. Probably it is.

Two of our daughters have suffered debilitating mental health problems in their teens and twenties. Perhaps this would have happened anyway. Who can be sure? But perhaps, if I had not been so anxious about Martha, I might at least have noticed the signs sooner. Good parenting is about paying attention. When one of your children has very obvious additional needs, it is easy to overlook the equally important needs of the others. It is easy to make mistakes.

There were impacts on our marriage too. This is not the place to go into details, but Adrian and I came perilously close to separation in the years after Martha was born. Again, some of this might have happened regardless, but the extra strains of having a disabled child undoubtedly played their part. Guilt, blame and grief all put additional pressure on any existing fault lines in a relationship. Thankfully we were supported to find our way through these difficulties. We were able to rebuild and strengthen our love for one another. But it was not easy.[32]

I believe that Martha is a gift and a blessing. She has made our family stronger and kinder. She is funny and charming and uniquely herself. None of us would choose to be without her. But the best gifts are always costly. No one learns to be patient or compassionate without being faced with some sort of trial or difficulty. Martha's special needs affected and continue to affect the whole family, for better and for worse.

This is my story. I cannot speak for my now-adult children. This section has been difficult to write, because I fear that I have failed them, often focusing too much on Martha's and my own needs, and too little on theirs. Perhaps I could have done better. If so, I am sorry.

But I would like to close this chapter with something positive. One lesson I have learned from Martha is that people are not to be valued in terms of their achievements. When children are doing well in school, getting high marks in exams, or succeeding at sports, we are ready with our praise and rewards. And rightly so; hard work should be encouraged. But the child who may never speak, or walk, or read or write is equally as precious as the one who wins all the prizes. I probably knew this theoretically before we had Martha. But it was only a year or more after her birth that I knew it with my heart.

Martha's needs undoubtedly put extra pressures on the whole family. But at the same time, I found myself beginning to relax my excessively high standards. I could loosen my grip on that need to be perfect. We were never going to be the perfect family now. Maybe the children wouldn't all get into top universities or have high-flying careers. Martha wouldn't be going to university at all, and that was ok. It didn't really matter in the end. None of us were perfect, me very much included. But we were all loved. We were all precious. We were all good enough, exactly as we were.

It took me a long time to understand this, but I believe this is the way God loves us all. None of us is accepted because we do or say or believe the right things. We are accepted because we are loved. That is enough, and it is everything.

People are not valuable because of what they can do, or what they know, or what they achieve. They are valuable because they are loved. Yes, of course I am proud and delighted when Martha makes advances in her speech or independence or understanding. But I am delighted with her exactly as she is, simply for being herself. And I am equally delighted with Adrian, and with all our other children too. Each one is a blessing and a gift.

Martha on holiday with some of her siblings

CHAPTER NINETEEN: SCHOOL DAYS

Martha started attending a local mainstream nursery shortly after her first birthday. The managers and staff could not have been more welcoming. Martha had a wonderful keyworker with whom she formed a close bond. Even though Martha could not crawl, let alone walk, she was supported to participate in a wide range of play activities. Using her trademark sideways bottom-shuffle, she quickly learned to move around with impressive speed when there were new toys to play with.

I was extremely grateful for the few hours of child-free time each week. After the intensity of Martha's first year, I was beginning to find a little breathing space for myself.

Another local nursery specialised in supporting children with additional needs to play and learn alongside typically developing children. This was a little pre-school in a rather scruffy church hall. But the moment you stepped inside you knew this place was special. It was run and managed by an inspirational lady who was passionate about welcoming all children, whatever their abilities. Her smile made me feel safe and warm. She helped me find a lovely volunteer to support Martha in this setting until we could access state funding. Soon Martha was enjoying messy play, music sessions and eating marmite on toast with her new friends. She was growing and learning every day.

At home we had a specialist teacher and a support worker who visited regularly to help with Martha's educational development. Often it was incredibly frustrating. Martha spent a lot of time throwing laminated picture cards onto the floor and generally refusing to engage. Children with Down Syndrome go through periods when they seem to be gaining new skills quite quickly. But then they will appear to stagnate, often for months at a time, seeming to learn nothing new.[33] I think in fact Martha was and is learning all the time, but she is frequently reluctant to demonstrate her abilities on request.

Children with Down Syndrome tend to have a strong dislike of failure, and Martha is no exception.[34] This means she will frequently refuse to try new things until she is certain she can get it right. And no amount of coaxing, bribes or threats will persuade Martha to do something she has made up her mind not to do. So educational toys were frequently flung away across the room until Martha was ready to deal with them on her own terms. Later she would amaze us with her ability to match the words to the pictures or fit the shapes into the slots as if we were wasting her time with such trivial tasks.

Martha, now aged fourteen, continues to learn on her own terms. From a baby who seemed so weak and vulnerable she has grown into a teenager whose capabilities continue to surprise us. One day she will be asking me to butter her toast because it is too difficult for her. But the next morning I will come down to the kitchen to find she has made herself a complete packed lunch, including jam sandwiches cut neatly into triangles and a packet of crisps from the high cupboard where I thought she couldn't find them.

Maratha loves swimming and yoga. She has recently started learning to play the cello. Faced with a book from school, Martha will come up with endless prevarications and excuses as to why she can't read it. But she has recently acquired a mobile phone. Suddenly she is writing long text messages to her siblings and reading their replies with little difficulty. Once Martha can see a direct benefit for herself, she produces abilities that she has been adept at hiding.

There is much discussion around the pros and cons of mainstream or special school settings for children with Down Syndrome. Initially we believed mainstream was the way to go. It seemed like the theoretical 'right' option, with research evidence to back it up.[35] I felt we were doing our bit for the principle of inclusion. If Martha's typically developing peers learned and played with Martha at school, this would help them become more accepting of people with disabilities.

So Martha started school at our local infant school,

where some of our older children had attended. She was made very welcome there, and enjoyed playing with toys in the reception class. But the pace of the school curriculum accelerates rapidly once children enter years one and two. Martha received one-to-one support and was given activities suitable for her abilities, but soon she began running off down the school corridors and hiding under the tables. She found the more formal learning environment too challenging, and responded by disengaging.

I found mainstream school for Martha difficult too. Perhaps I imagined it, but I felt a barrier of difference between myself and the other parents. Martha was rarely invited to birthday parties, and never to another child's home to play. I didn't really make friends with any of the other mothers; there was an awkwardness between us.

I was the mother who had to take my child into the classroom before the bell rang because Martha had wet herself on the way to school. I was the mother whose child sat down in the playground and refused to walk home. I was the one with the disabled child; the one whom nobody knew quite how to speak to. No one was unkind. No one said anything negative. Perhaps I imagined it. But I felt I did not belong.

And so, by the time Martha was seven, we transferred her to a local school for children with moderate special needs. It wasn't easy to do. It took months to convince the Local Authority that Martha's needs were not being met at the mainstream school. Then, once she had started at her new school, it took many more months, detailed legal research and the advice of a specialist solicitor before Martha won the entitlement to free school transport. Sometimes it takes fierce determination and brutal willpower to fight for Martha's rights. I worry about families who may not have the time, energy, or resources to fight.

But for Martha it was all worthwhile. Martha has been at her special needs school for almost eight years now, and she loves it. Her independence and social skills have blossomed, and she has some wonderful friendships. She missed school terribly during the first Covid 19 lockdown. During the later lockdowns I got determined again and insisted that Martha continue to attend school. Her happy, confident smiles on seeing her teachers and friends again told me I had made the right decision.

I could talk for hours about Martha's personality: her charm, her stubbornness, her sneaky ways of getting her own way, and her intuitive kindness. She gives the best hugs in the world. But I will close this section by sharing some things that Martha's friends have said about her.

One day at school, Martha's teacher asked all the children to say something positive about each member of the class. Their answers were written up on the whiteboard.

Martha's friends say she is helpful, funny, positive, happy, playful, caring, shy, nice, joyful and my best friend. She also has a beautiful smile.

All of this is true. I am so proud of Martha. She is my

beloved daughter.

Karen and Martha celebrating a school award

Martha as described by her school friends

CHAPTER TWENTY: WE ARE ALL DISABLED

There is an old Chinese story about cracked pots. You might have heard it before. A peasant farmer walks down the hill to the river every day to collect water. She carries two clay water jars hanging from a pole across her shoulders. One of the jars is cracked. As the old woman carries the water back up the hill, water leaks from the cracked pot. Where the water trickles out, beautiful flowers spring up. The woman refuses to exchange her cracked pot for a new one because she loves the flowers which grow beside her path.

Someone told me that story when Martha was just a couple of weeks old. I wasn't impressed. Don't try to fob me off with your shallow sentimentality, I thought.

Before Martha was born, I thought life was about striving for perfection. I didn't want any cracked pots, thank you. I worked hard to ensure my house was attractive and my children did well in school. My religion was neat and tidy. I tended to avoid people who looked odd or different.

Of course, we had problems and setbacks before Martha arrived. But I had always believed we could recover, start again, and restore perfection. But Martha was different; here was something fundamentally broken, a defective baby, delivered right into the heart of my home. It was as if a bomb had exploded. Nothing could be the same after this.

So I searched frantically for escape routes. Maybe we could give her away, maybe I could even kill her, maybe she wouldn't really have Down Syndrome. Only once all these options proved impossible did I begin to wrestle with the reality. My family was imperfect now. Who did that make me?

I kept trying to understand where God was in all this mess. How could he want people to be born with disabilities? Why did he let this happen? I kept pondering that picture I had imagined, of Mary, Joseph, and baby Jesus all with Down Syndrome. And, slowly, it helped me see things from a different perspective.

In the Christmas story, the inconceivably vast and powerful being of God somehow allows himself to be born as a baby in a cowshed.[36] Imagine you are all-seeing and all-knowing. You control the entire universe. Suddenly you become a human baby. You cannot speak, or walk, or care for yourself. Even your vision is limited to the floating shapes of your mother's face and a blur beyond. You are dependent on your peasant parents for your food, your warmth, and your very survival.

You have travelled from omnipotence to utter help-lessness.[37] Would it make very much difference if you also had Down Syndrome, or some other disability? I don't think so.

The distance between God and a human being is immense. It is mind-boggling. The distance between a typically developing person and someone with a disability is tiny by comparison. Even as healthy adults, we are all hopelessly limited. To be human is to have a fragile, aging body. Even the fittest among us is vulnerable to injury. Even our cleverest geniuses have blind spots and make mistakes. And however hard we try, we never seem able to become as good, as kind, as unselfish as we would like to be. We are all broken.

I am no theologian, but I think one of the lessons we can learn from the idea of God as a peasant baby is to accept our own vulnerability. If God can be so small, then perhaps small and damaged things can be beautiful and precious. Holy, even.

I think Jesus might just as well have had Down Syndrome; it would have made no great difference. Some people might find this shocking. But to me the real shock lies in the idea that God can be human, with all the limitations that entails.[38] If God can be as weak as a human baby, the small additional weakness of disability seems like nothing. To be human is to be disabled. We are all disabled.

I came, in my own time, to accept the lesson of the

cracked pot. Yes, the broken people do have capacity to bring immense sweetness and joy into all our lives. We can learn to appreciate them as a blessing. But I would go further. All the pots are cracked. None of us is whole or perfect; some of us just leak a little more than others.

I do not know why God allows pain and suffering. I do not understand, not really, why we are all so broken, so damaged. I am well aware that many people suffer loss and grief compared to which my difficulties over Martha are trivial. And I cannot say anything about that.

But what I hold onto is that, in some mysterious way, God joins us in our pain. He doesn't sit aloof in his heaven. He is not distant, or uncaring, or unconcerned. He has come to be part of our disabled world. He is one of us. He is a baby with Down Syndrome too.

My personal faith has become focused increasingly on the brokenness and the pain of God, especially in the life of Jesus. In the Gospels, Jesus consistently rejects power whenever it is offered. He hangs out with damaged people - the misfits, the sinners, the diseased and the disabled. He takes a child in his arms and says,

'Whoever welcomes in my name one of these children, welcomes me.'[39]

I like to imagine that the child Jesus was talking about had Down Syndrome.

Perhaps she did.

Martha aged four

CHAPTER TWENTY-ONE: LETTING THE LIGHT IN

The ancient Japanese art of *kintsugi* honours imperfection. When a ceramic pot or bowl is broken, it is painstakingly repaired with gold. The cracks become beautiful, giving the pot a new beginning. Kintsugi is a metaphor for life itself, paying visible tribute to the ways in which pain and loss can make us more resilient and more characterful.[40]

When Martha was born, I thought my life was over. Endless dreary years of being a carer stretched out in front of me. I felt as if nothing positive would ever happen to me ever again. My carefully curated world was smashed to pieces.

But those pieces became an opportunity. In the fourteen and a half years since Martha's arrival, my life has been filled with new adventures. After those early months and years, once Martha was happily settled in nursery and then in school, I began to test new passions, to take risks and try new experiences.

I took up running and completed several half marathons and other distance events. This gave me the confidence to sign up for karate classes. After years of determined effort, I eventually gained the last belt before black belt. I plunged into outdoor swimming and have come, weirdly, to love jumping into cold lakes and rivers.

I ran my own small business as a baby signing teacher. I volunteered at a local retreat centre. I studied for a diploma in art history. Once Martha was in full time school I went back to university and spent three years training to be a midwife. I travelled to the Philippines to discover midwifery practice in another culture. I achieved a first-class degree and went on to work as a midwife in London. Later I studied for another year to become a health visitor.

Yoga became another passion. I trained as a yoga teacher and once again set up my own small business, helping people find peace and calm through yoga, meditation, and reflexology. I built my own yoga and therapy studio in my garden.

Adrian and I have hiked long distance paths in many parts of Europe. We completed the last 100km of the Camino de Santiago together. This year we walked the South Downs Way, and we are already planning our next adventure.

Since the Covid 19 pandemic I have taken up writing. So far, I have completed one and a half novels in draft, and published a book about self care, *Finding Your Calm Space*. This book about Martha is my second published book.

At the time of writing this, I am working as a health professional on the Covid 19 vaccinations programme. I hugely enjoy meeting new people at the vaccination centres every day. It is a privilege to be part of a fantastic team.

Through all my adventures, I have made some remarkable friendships. I have been bowled over by people who are outstandingly generous, talented, fascinating, and kind. Many of them are the different, unusual sort of people I might have steered clear of before having Martha. Today I am honoured to call some of these people my dearest friends.

I have no desire to boast about my achievements. None of these things could have happened without the help of an amazing array of teachers, helpers, encouragers, and friends. And above all my family. Adrian and my children have supported me unstintingly and made so many dreams possible. We have also been greatly blessed with good health and financial security. I am well aware that not everyone enjoys these benefits. I am deeply grateful.

Of course, there are plenty of things I have *not* done. I have not persevered long term in a demanding senior career role. In fact, you could call me a bit of a butterfly, quickly moving on to the next challenge, the new adventure. I have not started a charity or inspired a movement. I never did get that karate black belt. And I have never run a marathon.

But I have had an enormous amount of fun. After that difficult first year or two, having a disabled child has inspired me to seize life in both hands. I have learned that I can survive setbacks and emerge stronger. As a family we have become creative and resourceful. We find ways of making things work.

Martha herself is my first inspiration. She has never allowed a little thing like Down Syndrome to prevent her from living her best life. Whether it is her favourite snacks, the attention of her siblings, or a new Spiderman accessory, Martha finds ways to get what she wants. She does this quietly, doggedly, and with remarkable intelligence. She doesn't waste time complaining if things get cancelled or plans change. She simply shrugs her shoulders and makes the most of whatever the day brings.

I have noticed that many parents of children with special needs like to run marathons, start new businesses or write poetry. I suspect facing challenge and limitation often inspires people to make the most of fresh opportunities. We learn to be more positive and perhaps to take more (calculated) risks. We become stronger and more resilient. We discover that life is far from perfect, but it is all the more worth living.

Looking to the future, there will doubtless be new challenges ahead. We do not know what Martha's next destination will be when she finishes school in a few years' time. We anticipate that our other children will soon all be largely independent of us, but Martha is likely to need our care and support for many years to come. This inevitably places some limitations on our plans for the next stage of our lives.

But we have learned that limitations can be worked around and creative solutions found. And we look forward to the immense joys still to come of sharing life with Martha. I anticipate plenty more adventures ahead.

Everyone's circumstances are different, and I appreciate that in many ways we have had a comparatively easy time. But I would encourage any new parents of children with disabilities to look to the future with hope. You may not know it yet, but you and your child are more resourceful, more resilient, and more beautiful than you can imagine right now.

Before Martha, my life was carefully sealed up against the strange, the difficult, and the imperfect. I was like a dull pot or a closely shuttered window. Martha cracked me apart and let the light in. I will be forever grateful.

A kintsugi bowl

Martha always knows how to enjoy life

POSTSCRIPT: TO TEST OR NOT TO TEST?

I have included this section as a Postscript because it is the fruit of long years of reflection, rather than my immediate experience. It is also longer than the other chapters. It may read a bit more like an essay and less like a story. However, it is still very much my personal and current thoughts. I hope it will provide some interesting ideas for consideration.

People often ask me whether I had the tests for Down Syndrome during my pregnancy. I didn't. It seemed like a simple decision at the time, but later, after everything that happened, I reflected deeply on this choice.

Adrian and I had always been opposed to abortion. We were Christians. We believed that human life began at conception and that killing was wrong. We supported some pro-life groups, making regular donations to their funds. It seemed quite straightforward back then.

In 2006, when I was pregnant with Martha, pregnant women in the UK were offered a nuchal translucency scan and a blood test at around twelve weeks. These screening tests are used to calculate a percentage probability that the foetus might have Down Syndrome. If that probability is high, more tests are then offered to get a more certain result. If the baby turns out to have Down Syndrome, termination of pregnancy is an option.[41] Today there are also more accurate blood tests available, but these did not exist in 2006.[42]

I said 'no thank you' to the twelve-week screening tests in all my pregnancies. I reasoned that, even if the probability of my baby having Down Syndrome turned out to be high, I would not opt for the amniocentesis test which carried a risk of miscarriage. And I would not want an abortion. So what would be the point in putting myself through all that worry?

We did opt for the twenty-week ultrasound scan for all our babies. To be honest, this was mostly for the excitement of seeing my growing baby on the screen and getting some of those blurry black and white photos to take home. But I was aware that this scan also looked for problems.

It was at the twenty-week scan that I got my first hint that there might be a problem with Martha. I went for the appointment on my own; we were old hands at this, and Adrian couldn't easily take the time off work. The sonographer spread the slimy gel on my belly and slid her transducer around. My baby's spine and head and heartbeat appeared on the screen, all in the right places. I smiled with satisfaction. But then the sonographer mentioned that my baby had some extra fluid on her kidneys.

'Oh. Is that a problem? What does it mean?', I asked.

'Well … It's probably nothing serious. I'll book you in for another scan at thirty-six weeks to check again. It can sometimes be a soft marker for Down Syndrome. But I shouldn't worry too much if I were you.'

So I didn't worry too much. The trained professional had told me not to, after all. She hadn't sounded too concerned. A 'soft marker' didn't sound so terrible. It was probably nothing.

I enjoyed my pregnancy. This would be the last time I would have a baby inside me. It was special. I loved feeling her turn and dance in my belly. I loved listening to the patter of her heartbeat at my midwife appointments. I even considered paying for one of those private '3D' scans. Wouldn't it be lovely to see my baby's face before she was born?

With hindsight this feels like a close call. There was probably a good chance that the private sonographer would have detected Martha's Down Syndrome, and I assume she would have been ethically bound to tell us about it. I could so easily have paid all that money for the special treat of seeing my unborn baby in colour and 3D, only to be told that she had an abnormality. My exciting day out would have turned into a nightmare.

I went back for the NHS scan at thirty-six weeks. My baby looked huge now, almost ready to be born. There was still a little extra fluid in her kidneys. The sonographer said she should get a kidney scan after she was born, but it was probably nothing too serious.

'So, is my baby all right?', I asked. 'Does everything else look normal?'

Perhaps I imagined it, but I thought she hesitated before replying, just for a moment.

'Well', she said, 'You'll be seeing this baby in a few weeks' time anyway.'

She hadn't answered my question, and I couldn't quite bring myself to ask her again.

I have often wondered: did that sonographer see signs of Down Syndrome but decide not to tell me? She could not have been certain; the paediatricians weren't even certain after Martha was born. Legally, if I had found out my baby had Down Syndrome, even at thirty-six weeks, I could have requested a termination of pregnancy. I don't think I would have done so, but my sonographer could not have known that. I have often wondered what she noticed, and what thoughts went through her mind.

Did she have doubts? Did she weigh up the ethics of telling me something, or keeping quiet? Was she trying to spare me? I will never know.

Over the months and years since Martha's birth I sometimes asked myself whether I should have had the prenatal tests for Down Syndrome. Would it have helped to have found out sooner? So many people seemed surprised that I had not had the tests. Perhaps I should have done? Would I have been better prepared?

When Martha was six years old, I started training to become a midwife. As a student, and then a midwife, I met hundreds of pregnant women. Part of my job was to offer them those tests. Most mums-to-be said 'yes', with little apparent thought.

Midwives are very busy, and the screening tests are part of the routine offer of antenatal care. If a woman declines the tests you have to make sure she properly understands what she is doing. You make careful notes; it is out of the ordinary. You would get into trouble as a midwife if a woman missed those tests by mistake. It can feel easier and safer if they just say yes.

Healthcare professionals are mostly kind and caring people. But they work under constant threat of litigation. As a midwife you quickly learn to err on the side of caution. If somebody gets a 'higher chance' result from the Down Syndrome twelve-week tests, she will be invited to see the specialist screening midwife. That midwife will have to tell the pregnant woman and her partner all the possible health and behaviour problems that their baby-to-be might have. It is a long list of negatives. Most children with Down Syndrome do not have every possible problem, but there is no way of knowing, not even from a full chromosome test, what each baby's particular future strengths and weaknesses might be.

If the screening midwife misses out one of the

negatives, and the baby turns out to have that particular issue, maybe those parents might sue her. But the midwife is under no compulsion to say that this child might turn out to be kind, or gentle, or artistic. She can't tell the parents that their child might one day hug them better than anyone else, or love animals, or dance beautifully at parties. She has to point out all the problems, and then send the parents away to make their difficult choice. The system seems to be biased against a more positive, or even neutral, approach to Down Syndrome.[43]

In the final year of my midwifery degree, I chose to study an optional module on health screening. It was a topic that troubled me, and so I seized the opportunity to explore it in more depth. I found it fascinating.

I learned that, contrary to some popular views, testing an apparently well population for a health condition is fraught with ethical dilemmas. Yes, you may find some curable problems and save some lives. But you may also stir up untold fear, anxiety and worry, often needlessly. You may invasively and unnecessarily treat people who would never actually have become ill with the condition in question. And you may give others false reassurance that they do not have the condition, when in fact they do.[44]

The UK National Screening Committee is tasked with determining which health screening programmes should be offered to UK populations. It publishes criteria which are supposed to underpin this difficult responsibility.[45] I discovered that screening for Down Syndrome does not sit comfortably within these ethical criteria.

For a screening programme to be approved, there must be, among other things, an effective intervention available. It would be wrong to test people for a condition if nothing could be done about it. This is how the National Screening Committee puts it:

'*There should be an effective intervention for patients identified through screening, with evidence that intervention at a pre-symptomatic phase leads to better outcomes for the screened individual compared with usual care. Evidence relating to wider benefits of screening, for example those relating to family members, should be taken into account where available. However, where there is no prospect of benefit for the individual screened then the screening programme should not be further considered.*'

Now this raises some tricky questions. Who is the individual being screened for Down Syndrome? The foetus, or the mother? If it is the foetus, the only possible intervention is termination. Is anyone suggesting that this is a benefit for that foetus? Would anyone want screening for, say, breast cancer, if the only treatment on offer was euthanasia?

The National Screening Committee guidance goes on to imply that the person being screened in the case of prenatal diagnoses is in fact the mother, and that the aim is to allow her to make an 'informed choice'. Even if this rather awkward rationalisation is accepted, I still struggle to make the next paragraph fit with screening for Down Syndrome:

'The benefit gained by individuals from the screening programme should outweigh any harms, for example from overdiagnosis, overtreatment, false positives, false reassurance, uncertain findings and complications.'

Do the benefits from screening for Down Syndrome outweigh the harms? This is at best debatable. Many parents feel they are not given helpful or balanced counselling after receiving test results. Some healthy babies are lost due to miscarriages resulting from amniocentesis or chorionic villus sampling tests. And parents-to-be suffer enormous amounts of stress, fear and anxiety when they receive positive test results. There are worries over false positive results from prenatal screening tests. The presentation and marketing of 'Non-Invasive Prenatal Testing' or NIPT tests to understandably anxious families has given rise to some serious ethical concerns.[46]

And then there is the impact on society's attitudes towards people with Down Syndrome. I understand the argument for choice. But when all pregnant mothers are routinely offered screening for a condition for which the only possible intervention is termination of pregnancy, this inevitably sends a negative message about that condition. The offer implies that you might wish to end the life of a child with Down Syndrome before that life begins. Perhaps it even suggests that this would be the responsible, the right thing to do. It tells me that people with Down Syndrome must somehow be sub-standard, a problem, perhaps best eliminated. Is this acceptable in a society where people with disabilities are supposed to have equal rights with everybody else?

I think this underlying message was one of the factors contributing to my deep feelings of guilt and shame when Martha was diagnosed. I had brought a child with Down Syndrome into the world. She was going to be a burden. It was my fault. No one ever said that I should have chosen the screening, should have aborted her. But every time anyone asked me if I had had the tests, I felt judged. I was expected to explain myself. It was uncomfortable every time.

Children with Down Syndrome and other disabilities do undoubtedly put additional pressures on their families and wider society. It would be wrong of me to trivialise this. In so many ways we have been lucky with Martha. At the time of writing, her health and behavioural problems are minimal. I know that is not true for all children with Down Syndrome. Adrian and I have a comfortable home, secure income, a supportive family. Many parents are not blessed with these advantages and will struggle to give their disabled children the extra care they need.

I should also add that the prenatal tests used to detect Down Syndrome also look for Edward's and Patau's Syndromes. These are much more severe conditions which usually result in profound disability and early death. I have huge sympathy with parents who receive these devastating diagnoses. I do not know what I would have done in their situation. It is possible to opt for screening only for these other syndromes and not for Down Syndrome.[47]

As a midwife, I cared for women whose babies had abnormalities. Some of them chose to terminate their pregnancies. I looked after mothers in labour with dead babies. I witnessed their pain and their grief. I sat beside some of these women while they cradled their lifeless children in their arms. The last thing I would wish to do is to judge or condemn any parent who makes the incredibly difficult decision to end a pregnancy in these horrendous circumstances. These are seriously tough choices. There are no painless answers.

It is not for me to tell anyone else what to do. I am not a lawmaker. I am not a judge. I believe in tolerance, kindness, and compassion. But I would encourage you to reflect deeply on these issues. Because they are important, for all of us. Our beliefs and choices about these matters impact on what sort of people we become, and on the kind of society we choose to build for one another.

For myself, after long reflection, I am glad that I chose not to have prenatal screening when I was pregnant with Martha.

Yes, in some ways we might have been better prepared. We could have done more research sooner. We could have braced ourselves for what was to come. I would not have gone through that awful experience of finding out in the days after Martha was born.

But it is never easy finding out that your child has a disability. Not at any time. I have met families who did not realise their child had Down Syndrome until he or she was a year old, or even older, and it was pointed out by a well-meaning stranger. I cannot imagine how devastating that must have been. I was angry with Doctor Shah when he told me Martha's diagnosis. If I had found out sooner, I would just have been angry with someone else instead.

If prenatal screening had given me a 'high chance' result, I would have had the agonising decision whether or not to opt for further tests with their promise of near-certainty and their threat of miscarriage. I would have worried and wept and suffered all those months. It would have been a miserable pregnancy.

As it was, I had such a happy pregnancy with Martha. It was a precious time of joyful anticipation. I am glad no one took that away from me. Many people talk about pressures from health professionals to terminate a pregnancy once Down Syndrome or another condition has been detected.[48] This might have been a problem for me.

But to be honest, I think the biggest pressure would have come from myself. Until Martha was two or three months old, I fantasised about smothering her with a pillow. I had this massive urge somehow to get rid of this problem I could not yet accept. If I felt like this towards my living baby whom I held in my arms and fed at my breasts, how would I have coped with an offer of legal termination of pregnancy? Would I have had the strength to say no? I am far from certain.

Despite all my Catholic and Christian principles,

my long-held pro-life beliefs, I do not know how I would have coped with continuing my pregnancy, knowing my child had Down Syndrome. And therefore I am profoundly grateful that I did not know.

If I had ended that pregnancy, I would have had to live with the guilt of having gone against my own beliefs about human life before birth. That, I suspect, would have changed me for the worse.

But more than that, I would never have known Martha. I would never have known the deep sorrow and the amazing joy that she awoke in me. I would never have seen her beautiful smile, never felt her loving arms embracing me. I would not be able to walk away from my laptop now and spend the rest of my day with her. My world would be darker, sadder, poorer. I am so glad that Martha is here. She lets the light into my life every single day.

Our beautiful daughter

ABOUT THE AUTHOR

Karen Lawrence

Karen Lawrence is a mother of seven, yoga teacher and former midwife. She lives with her family in Billericay, Essex, UK.

When she is not working, writing or caring for her family, Karen enjoys open water swimming and hiking long trails with her husband. She is one of those crazy people who like to dip in icy lakes and rivers though the winter.

Karen loves writing. She writes haiku, short stories, blogs and the occasional longer poem. In 2020 she published a book about self-care entitled Finding Your Calm Space. She is currently working on two novels.

BOOKS BY THIS AUTHOR

Finding Your Calm Space

Life is stressful. Especially these days. Mental health statistics are soaring. Inflammatory disease is on the increase. Everyone needs calm in a crazy world.

My book Finding Your Calm Space offers you thirty-one simple ways to find calm for wellbeing, health and happiness. It is designed to be read over one month, discovering a new calming practice each day.

I share anecdotes from my wide experience of yoga teaching, parenting, reflexology and midwifery as I introduce each practice. Together we discover how to find calm through the body, the breath, the natural world, creativity and connection.

Most of the calm practices in this book can be done in just ten minutes. Each practice is explained in easy steps.

It's time to find your calm space.

FOOTNOTES AND FURTHER READING

---

[1]

You can read more about John Langdon Down and his work here:
    https://library.down-syndrome.org/en-us/research-practice/06/1/john-langdon-down-man-message

[2] You can read more about people first language and why it is important here:
    https://dsagsl.org/wp-content/uploads/2019/01/DSAGSL_LanguageGuide1.pdf

[3] A 'FISH' test is an acronym short for 'Fluorescent In Situ Hybridization'. This is a technique that can determine how many copies of a particular chromosome a cell has. It can therefore detect the presence of a third chromosome 21 which is the cause of Down Syndrome. Results are usually available in a few days. A full diagnosis of a chromosomal abnormality such as Down Syndrome will require karyotyping, where the cells are cultured and analysed in more detail, but this can take as long as a few weeks. You can read more here

if you are interested: https://www.verywellhealth.com/diagnosing-down-syndrome-1120396

[4] The UK Down's Syndrome Association is a wonderful organisation which does great work to support people with Down Syndrome and their families. You can learn much more about all aspects of Down Syndrome at their website:
https://www.downs-syndrome.org.uk/

[5] My local support group in Essex is called Down Syndrome Extra 21. They are a marvellous and friendly group of parents who organise a wide range of social and informational events to support families and people with DS. Their website is:
https://www.extra21.org.uk/about

[6] A health visitor is a specialist nurse or midwife who supports the health and wellbeing of young children in the community. Sadly, the scope of health visitors' work in England has been much diminished in recent years due to changes in commissioning and funding. Our health visitor was a great support to me at this crucial time.

[7] SNAP stands for Special Needs and Parents. You can learn more about this wonderful charity in Brentwood, Essex at their website:
https://www.snapcharity.org/

[8] Heidi Crowter has recently challenged current UK law regarding termination of pregnancy where the foetus has Down Syndrome. Heidi has Down Syndrome herself. You can read more here about her court case:
https://righttolife.org.uk/news/woman-with-downs-syndrome-takes-uk-govt-to-court-over-allow-

ing-abortion-up-to-birth-for-disabilities

https://www.theguardian.com/society/2021/jul/06/downs-syndrome-sajid-javid-court-abortion-law-heidi-crowter

[9] Welcome to Holland is a poem by Emily Perl Kingsley. Many people find it helpful, although I did not. You can access a copy here:

https://www.dsasc.ca/uploads/8/5/3/9/8539131/welcome_to_holland.pdf

[10] There is lots of excellent scientific evidence for the health and developmental benefits of breast milk. See for example

https://www.unicef.org.uk/babyfriendly/news-and-research/baby-friendly-research/infant-health-research/infant-health-research-brain-and-cognitive-development/

[11] The Royal College of Paediatrics and Child Health (RCPCH) produces growth charts which are used widely in the UK to enable parents and health professionals to ensure that children are growing normally. The charts feature centile lines indicating statistical norms for healthy development. Babies and children usually more or less follow one of these lines as they grow. It is a cause for concern if a baby's weight either drops down or climbs up one or more centiles. Children with Down Syndrome have a different normal growth trajectory from other children, so specialised charts should be used. You can read more about this at:

https://www.rcpch.ac.uk/resources/uk-who-growth-charts-down-syndrome-0-18-years

[12] An echocardiogram is a specialised ultrasound scan of the heart. You can learn more about this here: https://www.nhs.uk/conditions/echocardiogram/

[13] Martha's heart problem was a ventricular septal defect, or VSD for short. You can learn more about a VSD here: https://chfed.org.uk/how-we-help/information-service/heart-conditions/ventricular-septal-defect-vsd/

[14] Baptist Christians believe that baptism should not be given to infants but should be reserved for adults who have made their own profession of faith. Instead of baptising babies, Baptists usually have a service of dedication, where the parents promise to bring up their child in the Christian faith and ask for God's blessing on their family. You can read more about this here: https://www.baptist.org.uk/Publisher/File.aspx?ID=168468&view=browser

[15] Scripture quotation from Revised Standard Version of the Bible—Second Catholic Edition (Ignatius Edition) Copyright © 2006 National Council of the Churches of Christ in the United States of America. Used by permission. All rights reserved worldwide.

[16] A naso-gastric feeding tube, or NG tube for short, is a plastic tube inserted through the patient's nose down into the stomach. It enables feeds to be given directly and is often used to support children and other people who are failing to gain weight. You can read more here: https://www.dbth.nhs.uk/wp-content/uploads/2017/07/wpr42300-nasogastric-feeding-tube-info-

for-parents.pdf

[17] In 2007 the internet was full of suggestions about the benefits of various dietary supplements for babies with Down Syndrome. Clinical trials later demonstrated that these expensive treatments had no demonstrable benefits.
https://www.sciencedaily.com/releases/2008/02/080223123616.htm

[18] Martha received outstanding care at the Royal Brompton Hospital in London which has pioneered life-saving heart surgery for decades. We are incredibly grateful to the hospital and the NHS for the brilliant care she was given throughout. At no point did we feel that her diagnosis of Down Syndrome in any way impacted on the quality of her care. She was treated consistently with respect, kindness, and top-quality care. Thank you!
https://www.rbht.nhs.uk/our-hospitals

[19] Temporary pacing wires are used routinely in the immediate phase of recovery after cardiac surgery to correct any post-operative disturbances in heart rhythms. You can read more about this here if you are interested:
https://www.ncbi.nlm.nih.gov/pmc/articles/PMC2840753/

[20] Madeleine McCann has never been found. You can read more about her family's heart-breaking story here:
https://en.wikipedia.org/wiki/Disappearance_of_Madeleine_McCann

[21] OT is short for Occupational Therapist. These professionals help children with learning disabilities develop skills to access a wide range of day-to-day activities. You can read more here:

https://www.nelft.nhs.uk/services-essex-childrens-occupational-therapy/

[22] Physio is shorthand for a physiotherapist. These professionals helped Martha with her motor skills and physical development. You can read more here:

https://www.shb.scot.nhs.uk/departments/physiotherapy/APCP-DownSyndrome.pdf

[23] You can learn more about the diversity of people with Down Syndrome here:

http://www.intellectualdisability.info/diagnosis/articles/downs-syndrome

[24] The language we use when talking about people with disabilities is important. I may not always have got it 100% right in this book, but I have tried my best. I think the most important thing is to remember that people with disabilities are people first. Disability should not define anyone. You can read about a recent project to encourage respectful and helpful language when referring to people with Down Syndrome here:

https://www.languagecreatesreality.com/

[25] There is a Flemish painting depicting a nativity scene where one of the angels and one of the shepherds have the features of people with Down Syndrome. This picture is very dear to me. I have a copy on the wall of my study.

http://www.downssideup.com/2012/12/a-christmas-angel-with-down-syndrome.html

[26] Confession, or the Sacrament of Reconciliation as practiced by Roman Catholics is a much-misunderstood practice. Like all encounters involving trust, it is of course open to misuse. I find it difficult to share my innermost feelings of inadequacy, so I frequently find excuses to put off going to confession. But my personal experience is that I have never regretted the release and comfort of speaking my sorrow and hearing my forgiveness spoken aloud. Often it has helped me break through difficult barriers in my life and personal growth.

You can learn more about this here:

https://www.catholicscomehome.org/your-questions/what-is-the-sacrament-of-confession/

[27] Rett Syndrome is a rare neurological disorder affecting mainly females. You can learn more about it here:

https://www.rettuk.org/what-is-rett-syndrome/

[28] Hearing loss and recurrent ear infections are common problems for children with Down Syndrome. You can read more about this here:

https://www.ndcs.org.uk/information-and-support/childhood-deafness/causes-of-deafness/downs-syndrome/

[29] Grommets are tiny tubes inserted into the eardrums to equalise pressure inside the ears. The operation is done under a general anaesthetic. You can read more about grommets here:

https://www.gosh.nhs.uk/conditions-and-treatments/procedures-and-treatments/treatment-glue-ear-grommets/

[30] Makaton is used by over 100,00 children and adults either as their main method of communication or to support speech. You can learn more here:
https://makaton.org/TMC/About_Makaton/TMC/ AboutMakaton.aspx?hkey=c8a4263d-78cc-4c30- b135-153eb6ac3118

[31] The siblings of children with special needs have particular needs and vulnerabilities of their own, as well as opportunities for personal growth. You can read more about this here:
https://www.sibs.org.uk/supporting-young-sib- lings/professionals/needs-of-young-siblings/

[32] Many couples with a child with a learning dis- ability report additional strains on their relationships. You can read more about this here:
https://www.relate.org.uk/sites/default/files/the_ way_we_are_now_-_under_pressure_report_0.pdf

[33] Children with Down Syndrome seem to have some identifiable learning patterns. You can read more about this here:
https://specialreads.com/intuit-your-childs-learn- ing-style-pass-it-on/

[34] Educational strategies for children with Down Syndrome need to allow for a common tendency to avoid the risk of failure:
https://library.down-syndrome.org/en-gb/re- search-practice/07/2/motivation-learning-styles-young- down-syndrome/

[35] Some studies suggest that children with Down Syndrome may do better in a mainstream setting. In

practice this will depend on the particular child and the educational options available. You can read more about this here:

https://library.down-syndrome.org/en-gb/news-update/06/1/inclusive-education-individuals-down-syndrome/

[36] You can read more here about the Christian belief that God became man in Jesus. This is known as the Incarnation.

https://www.christianity.com/wiki/holidays/how-was-jesus-god-incarnate.html

[37] God's humility is a theme found in many places in the Bible. You can read about this in Philippians 2 verses 3-8 and 1 Corinthians 1 verses 18-29.

[38] Christians often struggle with the idea that Jesus could be truly human. This is a helpful article on this topic:

https://www.desiringgod.org/articles/jesus-is-fully-human

[39] Mark 9 verse 37

Scriptures and additional materials quoted are from the Good News Bible © 1994 published by the Bible Societies/HarperCollins Publishers Ltd UK, Good News Bible© American Bible Society 1966, 1971, 1976, 1992. Used with permission.

[40] You can learn more about the art of kintsugi here:

https://esprit-kintsugi.com/en/quest-ce-que-le-kintsugi/

[41] You can read more about pre-natal testing for

Down Syndrome and other chromosomal abnormalities here:

https://www.nhs.uk/pregnancy/your-pregnancy-care/screening-for-downs-edwards-pataus-syndrome/

[42] Nowadays there is also the option of a blood test which gives a more accurate result than the standard twelve-week screening test. This is known as a NIPT test. These tests are available on the NHS after a positive twelve-week screening test, but they are also heavily marketed to pregnant women by private providers. You can read more here:

https://www.nuh.nhs.uk/about-the-nipt-

[43] The Down's Syndrome Association provides an excellent free webinar called *Tell it Right*. This is designed to help midwives and other health professionals present information about Down Syndrome to pregnant couples and new parents. It includes balanced information about living with Down Syndrome and parents' perspectives. You can find this material here:

https://www.downs-syndrome.org.uk/our-work/services-projects/training/tell-it-right-webinar-for-maternity-services-and-universities/

[44] All health screening tests have benefits and risks. More screening is not always better. You can read more about this here:

https://www.ncbi.nlm.nih.gov/books/NBK279418/

[45] You can read the UK National Screening Committee's criteria here: https://www.gov.uk/government/publications/evidence-review-criteria-national-screening-programmes/criteria-for-appraising-the-viability-effectiveness-and-appropriateness-of-a-screening-

programmetest/

[46] The potential harms arising from testing and screening for Down Syndrome are manifold. You can read more about this at these links:

https://www.nuffieldbioethics.org/blog/nipt-private

https://www.downs-syndrome.org.uk/wp-content/uploads/2020/08/2020.FactChecker_NIPT.pdf

[47] You can read more about Edward's and Patau's Syndromes here:

https://www.gov.uk/government/publications/screening-tests-for-you-and-your-baby/downs-syndrome-edwards-syndrome-and-pataus-syndrome-combined-or-quadruple-test-taken-on-or-after-1-june-2021

[48] This recent BBC article describes the pressures experienced by some families on receiving a prenatal diagnosis of Down Syndrome:

https://www.bbc.co.uk/news/uk-england-beds-bucks-herts-51658631

Printed in Great Britain
by Amazon

71142313R00092